The Constitution and the Founding of America

Titles in the World History Series

WORLD
HISTORY SERIES

The Constitution and the Founding of America

by
Lydia Bjornlund

Lucent Books, P.O. Box 289011, San Diego, CA 92198-9011

Library of Congress Cataloging-in-Publication Data

Bjornlund, Lydia D.
    The Constitution and the founding of America/Lydia
      Bjornlund.
        p. cm.—(World history series)
    Includes bibliographical references and index.
    Summary: Discusses the United States Constitution and the
founding of America, covering such aspects as the Constitutional Convention, the writing of the Constitution, the struggle
for ratification, and the enduring legacy of this document.
    ISBN 1-56006-586-9 (lib. : alk. paper)
    1. United States Constitution—History—Juvenile literature.
2. United States—Politics and government—1775–1783—Juvenile
literature. 3. United States—Politics and government—1783–
1789—Juvenile literature. [1. United States—Constitutional
history. 2. United States—Politics and government—1775–
1783. 3. United States—Politics and government—1783–1789]
I. Title. II. Series.

E303.B66   2000
320.973'09'03321—dc21

                                                    99-039423

Contents

Foreword

Each year on the first day of school, nearly every history teacher faces the task of explaining why his or her students should study history. One logical answer to this question is that exploring what happened in our past explains how the things we often take for granted—our customs, ideas, and institutions—came to be. As statesman and historian Winston Churchill put it, "Every nation or group of nations has its own tale to tell. Knowledge of the trials and struggles is necessary to all who would comprehend the problems, perils, challenges, and opportunities which confront us today." Thus, a study of history puts modern ideas and institutions in perspective. For example, though the founders of the United States were talented and creative thinkers, they clearly did not invent the concept of democracy. Instead, they adapted some democratic ideas that had originated in ancient Greece and with which the Romans, the British, and others had experimented. An exploration of these cultures, then, reveals their very real connection to us through institutions that continue to shape our daily lives.

Another reason often given for studying history is the idea that lessons exist in the past from which contemporary societies can benefit and learn. This idea, although controversial, has always been an intriguing one for historians. Those who agree that society can benefit from the past often quote philosopher George Santayana's famous statement, "Those who cannot remember the past are condemned to repeat it." Historians who subscribe to Santayana's philosophy believe that, for example, studying the events that led up to the major world wars or other significant historical events would allow society to chart a different and more favorable course in the future.

Just as difficult as convincing students to realize the importance of studying history is the search for useful and interesting supplementary materials that present historical events in a context that can be easily understood. The volumes in Lucent Books' World History Series attempt to present a broad, balanced, and penetrating view of the march of history. Ancient Egypt's important wars and rulers, for example, are presented against the rich and colorful backdrop of Egyptian religious, social, and cultural developments. The series engages the reader by enhancing historical events with these cultural contexts. For example, in *Ancient Greece,* the text covers the role of women in that society. Slavery is discussed in *The Roman Empire,* as well as how slaves earned their freedom. The numerous and varied aspects of everyday life in these and other societies are explored in each volume of the series. Additionally, the series covers the major political, cultural, and philosophical ideas as the torch of civilization is passed from ancient Mesopotamia and Egypt, through Greece, Rome, medieval Europe, and other world cultures, to the modern day.

The material in the series is formatted in a thorough, precise, and organized manner. Each volume offers the reader a comprehensive and clearly written overview of an important historical event or period. The topic under discussion is placed in a broad, historical context. For example, *The Italian Renaissance* begins with a discussion of the High Middle Ages and the loss of central control that allowed certain Italian cities to develop artistically. The book ends by looking forward to the Reformation and interpreting the societal changes that grew out of the Renaissance. Thus, students are not only involved in an historical era, but also enveloped by the events leading up to that era and the events following it.

One important and unique feature in the World History Series is the primary and secondary source quotations that richly supplement each volume. These quotes are useful in a number of ways. First, they allow students access to sources they would not normally be exposed to because of the difficulty and obscurity of the original source. The quotations range from interesting anecdotes to farsighted cultural perspectives and are drawn from historical witnesses both past and present. Second, the quotes demonstrate how and where historians themselves derive their information on the past as they strive to reach a consensus on historical events. Lastly, all of the quotes are footnoted, familiarizing students with the citation process and allowing them to verify quotes and/or look up the original source if the quote piques their interest.

Finally, the books in the World History Series provide a detailed launching point for further research. Each book contains a bibliography specifically geared toward student research. A second, annotated bibliography introduces students to all the sources the author consulted when compiling the book. A chronology of important dates gives students an overview, at a glance, of the topic covered. Where applicable, a glossary of terms is included.

In short, the series is designed not only to acquaint readers with the basics of history, but also to make them aware that their lives are a part of an ongoing human saga. Perhaps they will then come to the same realization as famed historian Arnold Toynbee. In his monumental work, *A Study of History*, he wrote about becoming aware of history flowing through him in a mighty current, and of his own life "welling like a wave in the flow of this vast tide."

Important Dates in the History of the Constitution and the Founding of America

April 1775
First shots of the American Revolution are fired in Massachusetts.

July 1776
The Declaration of Independence is approved by Congress.

September 1783
Peace treaty is signed with British.

August 1786– February 1787
Shays's Rebellion occurs in western Massachusetts.

ca. 1775   1776   1777   1781   1783   1786

March 1781
Articles of Confederation are ratified by the states.

November 1777
Articles of Confederation are adopted by Continental Congress.

June 1775
George Washington assumes command of Continental forces.

September 1786
Annapolis convention is held; Hamilton proposes a convention to update the Articles of Confederation.

December 1787
Delaware becomes the first state to ratify the Constitution.

February 1787
Confederation Congress warily endorses convention "for the sole and express purpose of revising the Articles of Confederation."

June 1788
New Hampshire becomes the ninth state to ratify the Constitution, which is all that is needed for it to go into effect.

March 1789
First Congress holds its initial meeting in New York.

December 1789
The Bill of Rights is ratified, making it part of the U.S. Constitution.

1787	1788	1789	1790	1791

September 1787
Constitution signed by delegates at the convention.

April 1789
George Washington is inaugurated as president.

May 1790
Rhode Island becomes the last of the original thirteen states to sign the Constitution.

May 1787
Constitutional Convention opens in Philadelphia.

September 1789
Congress submits the Bill of Rights to the states.

Introduction

The American Experiment

The Constitution of the United States is the oldest document of its kind in the world. It has endured more than two centuries of changes as the country has grown from a tentative union of states to the most powerful nation in the world. The story of how this document was created is remarkable.

As a whole, the delegates to the Constitutional Convention of 1787 were well educated and experienced in government. Many had fought in the American Revolution and had represented their states in the First and Second Continental Congresses. Some had been involved in drafting the constitutions of their states and the Articles of Confederation. They brought their experience and skills to bear in drafting a unique and innovative document.

The framers of the Constitution had a vision of a government that would be responsive to the people. Their vision was of a government strong enough to meet the challenges the nation would face while protecting the individual liberties they had fought to achieve. John Rut-

George Washington presides over the Constitutional Convention in 1787.

ledge, a South Carolina delegate, proclaimed that the convention was "laying the foundation for a great empire."[1]

The strength and endurance of the Constitution stems from the ability of the delegates at the Constitutional Convention to consider both the past and the future. In drafting the document, they drew upon current knowledge and political theory, but they focused particular attention on the practical solutions that nations and states had derived to address common problems of governance. They borrowed the idea of a limited government from the Magna Carta and incorporated some of the restrictions on governmental power that had been put forth in England's 1689 Bill of Rights. They applied the principles of separate and balanced power from Charles de Montesquieu's writings and of popular sovereignty from John Locke's treatises. In addition, they borrowed heavily from their own experiences in drafting state constitutions. They applied the bicameral system of government, which was used by all states except Pennsylvania, and adopted the electoral college system used by the state of Maryland to resolve issues related to the election of the president.

The men at the Constitutional Convention were a product of their times. The American Revolution and events leading up to it had made them wary of a powerful government. But they also had experienced the inadequacies of the national government under the Articles of Confederation.

Thus, they looked for ways to empower the government to carry out the necessary business of the fledgling nation without enabling it to encroach on the rights of citizens. "In framing a government which is to be administered by men over men," wrote James Madison, "the great difficulty lies in this: you must first enable the government to control the governed, and in the next place oblige it to control itself."[2]

The framers of the Constitution were not convinced that they had developed a perfect system of government. They recognized that the nation was changing. Already, Americans were pushing beyond the boundaries of the thirteen original states. The delegates at the convention recognized that government would surely have questions and crises for which they could not predict answers and solutions. Thus, they built flexibility into the plans they had made; in areas about which they were unsure, they left the details to later generations to decide. The amendment process and other mechanisms built into the Constitution have enabled our republic to withstand the test of time and the stress of change.

Despite the lofty ideals that the Constitution espouses, it is a relatively simple document. Gouverneur Morris, who drafted the language of the document, wrote, "For my part, I think the whole of it is expressed in the plain, common language of mankind."[3] Written for a government by the people, of the people, and for the people, the Constitution is also wonderfully accessible to the people.

1 Settling the New World

The ideas that serve as the cornerstone of the U.S. Constitution were born long before the Constitution was written. The early immigrants to America brought across the Atlantic Ocean from Europe some of the political ideas that were later incorporated into the framework for a new government. They also brought a legacy of representative government; British Parliament was more than five hundred years old. As the colonies and colonists struggled to survive and thrive in the New World, written contracts were established to govern community behavior. These contracts paved the way for the U.S. Constitution.

During the century and a half that America consisted of British colonies, the colonists learned much about the nature of governance. By the time of the American Revolution, all thirteen of the colonies had elected assemblies that helped establish local rules and regulations. They learned the importance of representative government. In addition, as Englishmen, they believed in common law and the rights of men.

However, the colonists' experiences in a new land also caused them to have different ideas from England. According to English law, which was followed in the colonies, men who owned land had the right to vote and to hold office. Throughout the American colonies, land was used to entice new colonists to settle the territory. Thus, more people owned land in the colonies than in the mother country. And not all landowners were from wealthy, aristocratic families. Land was a great equalizer. As a result, a greater percentage of the population was eligible to vote and to hold office than in England. Many elected assemblies in the colonies also differed from England's Parliament in that each town sent a representative. Thus, the colonists developed a different opinion about what representative government meant. From this colonial experience grew the ideas and principles that were to serve as the cornerstones of the Constitution and the Bill of Rights.

IN SEARCH OF A NEW WORLD

A number of factors contributed to the decision of Europeans to migrate to the New World. Spain sent conquistadors to conquer new lands and mine the valuable metals. France sent explorers to claim new land and trappers and traders to exploit the fur trade. However, England's involvement in several wars during the fifteenth and sixteenth centuries had depleted the treasury, so England lacked the funds needed to launch such enterprises.

Thus, the English settlements in America began mainly as private enterprises. England's thirteen colonies in North America were founded by trading companies looking for wealth, by settlers attracted to the possibility of owning their own land, by reformers searching for a place to carry out their dreams of a perfect society, and by religious groups seeking shelter from persecution and harassment. The English government backed the efforts through written charters that gave private organizations the right to settle areas owned by England.

THE FIRST SETTLEMENTS

The Virginia Company of London, a group of investors, founded the first permanent English settlement in Jamestown, Virginia, in 1607. The investors had three principal objectives: to find a northwest water passage to the wealth of Asia, to exploit the gold and silver of America, and to find suitable lands for producing exotic crops such as silk or spices.

The colony in Virginia barely survived. Many of the settlers were members of the gentry, adventurers who were unused to hard work. They chased after an easy fortune in silver and gold rather than planting a harvest or searching for food. Sickness and starvation took a heavy toll, and only 38 of the original 144 settlers lived through the first winter. Captain

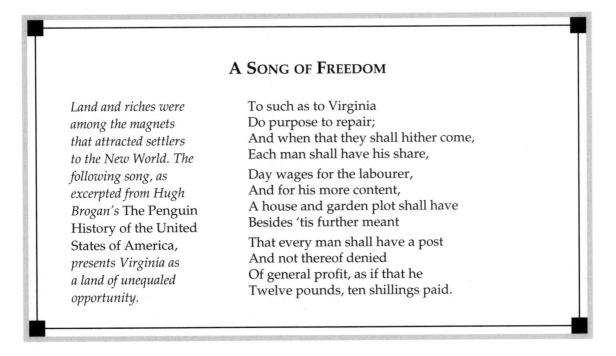

A SONG OF FREEDOM

Land and riches were among the magnets that attracted settlers to the New World. The following song, as excerpted from Hugh Brogan's The Penguin History of the United States of America, *presents Virginia as a land of unequaled opportunity.*

To such as to Virginia
Do purpose to repair;
And when that they shall hither come,
Each man shall have his share,

Day wages for the labourer,
And for his more content,
A house and garden plot shall have
Besides 'tis further meant

That every man shall have a post
And not thereof denied
Of general profit, as if that he
Twelve pounds, ten shillings paid.

Before the Pilgrims landed, they signed the Mayflower Compact, an agreement to live by a common set of rules.

John Smith, who had emerged as a leader, instituted a policy of rigid discipline, strengthened defenses, and encouraged farming with this admonishment: "He who does not work, will not eat."[4] When he left Virginia in 1609, Smith described the colony as "a miserie, a ruin, a death, a Hell."[5]

The Virginia Company recognized that the entire venture's success depended on its ability to attract artisans, laborers, fishermen, and farmers to the settlement. To attract new settlers, the company began to give away land—a commodity that was plentiful in the New World. Land became a magnet that attracted the kind of people who were firmly committed to making the community a success. Unlike the original settlers of Jamestown, later immigrants did not come expecting to make a quick profit and then return to England. They expected to make their home in the New World.

THE MAYFLOWER COMPACT

Among the new settlers that the Virginia Company convinced to move to the New World was a small group of English expatriates living in Holland. These people, the Pilgrims, were far different than the settlers of Jamestown. They were not in search of riches, but of a "city on a hill," an ideal community that all the world would admire. They wanted to live where their children would not be influenced by outside forces and where they could live according to the laws and customs of their Puritan religion.

In 1620, thirty-five Pilgrim men, women, and children set out across the Atlantic Ocean. Also on board were about sixty others—artisans, soldiers, and indentured servants who sought a new life in the New World. The Pilgrims called them "strangers."

The Pilgrims originally set sail for Virginia, but winds blew them off course. As they prepared to land at Plymouth in the Massachusetts Bay, some of the passengers declared that the contract that was to rule them in Virginia had no authority in this strange northern land. William Bradford, a leader of the Pilgrims, later recalled that the passengers threatened that when they "came ashore they would use their own liberty, for none had power to command them."[6]

Bradford and his colleagues were alarmed by this turn of events. They knew

A View from William Bradford

In their quest for a better community, the Pilgrims faced the unknown head-on, putting their faith in God to see to their safety. William Bradford was among the leaders during the voyage and the Pilgrims' first years in Plymouth. In this excerpt from On Plimouth Plantation, *Bradford describes what it was like to be a Pilgrim getting ready to disembark from the Mayflower.*

"Here I cannot but pause and stand amazed, and so, too, I think will the reader when he considers this poor people and their present condition. For they had no dwelling places for their weatherbeaten bodies; no houses or much less towns to repair to, to seek for succor. And for the season it was winter, and they that know the winters of that country [New England] know them to be sharp and violent, and subject to cruel and fierce storms, dangerous to travel to known places, much more to search an unknown coast. Besides what could they see but a hideous and desolate wilderness, full of wild beasts and wild men—and what multitudes there might be of them they knew not. Nor could they . . . view . . . a more goodly country to feed their hopes; for which way soever they turned their eyes (save upward to the heavens) they would have little solace or content in respect of any outward objects. For summer being done, all things stand upon them with a weatherbeaten face, and the whole country, full of woods and thickets represented a wild and savage hue. . . . If they looked behind them, there was the mighty ocean over which they had passed and was now a main bar and gulf to separate them from all the civil parts of the world. . . . What could now sustain them but the spirit of God and His Grace?"

William Bradford and other leaders among the Pilgrims created the Mayflower Compact.

that survival depended on orderly behavior as a community. Thus, they agreed to join in a covenant, much like the covenant that governed their church. Anchored offshore, they signed what has come to be known as the Mayflower Compact. The signers agreed to "covenant and combine ourselves together into a civil Body Politick, for our better Ordering and Preservation" and to make and abide by "Laws, Ordinances, Acts, Constitutions, and Officers, from time to time, as shall be thought most meet and convenient for the general Good of the Colony."[7] In effect, the Mayflower Compact was a revolutionary concept, establishing a government based on the consent of the governed.

The Mayflower Compact was the first of many self-governing agreements that were drafted of necessity as people settled in the New World. The idea that governments derive their power from the consent of the governed took root in the American mind. In 1682, when William Penn introduced the constitution for his colony, he explained, "Any government is free to the people under it (whatever be the frame) where the laws rule and the people are a party to those laws . . . for liberty without obedience is confusion, and obedience without liberty is slavery."[8]

Historian Hugh Brogan writes that the Mayflower Compact's example

> was unconsciously but exactly followed in seventeenth-century New England, in eighteenth-century Kentucky, throughout revolutionary America, and everywhere on the nineteenth-century frontier: in Texas, California, Iowa and Oregon. These agreements enabled generations of settlers to feel that their lives, property and prospects were secure under the rule of law. . . . All this prepared the way for the greatest compact of all, the Constitution of the United States.[9]

Like the creators of the Mayflower Compact almost two hundred years earlier, the people who signed the Constitution—representing "We, the people"—agreed to abide by its provisions.

THIRTEEN COLONIES EMERGE

The thirteen English colonies were not created according to a grand scheme. Like Virginia, most of the early colonies were founded by joint-stock trading companies. New York, for example, was founded by the Dutch West India Company in 1623. (New York was originally owned by Holland and called New Amsterdam.)

Although the Massachusetts Bay Colony was formed by Puritans fleeing religious persecution and harassment, it too was set up as a business venture. Rhode Island and Connecticut emerged from settlements that resulted primarily from people moving out of the Massachusetts Bay Colony.

Massachusetts was not the only colony formed as a refuge from persecution. In 1632, Lord Baltimore founded Maryland as a refuge for Roman Catholics. In 1681, William Penn led Quakers to Pennsylvania. The idea of creating a better life in America was not unique to religiously persecuted peoples. Over a century after the Puritans reached Massachusetts, James Oglethorpe founded Georgia as a haven where those in English debtor prisons and other convicts could start a new life.

COLONIAL GOVERNMENT

Despite their different origins, all the settlements had one thing in common—they needed a way to make decisions for the community. Throughout the colonies, representative assemblies grew up out of necessity. The first such elected body was the Virginia House of Burgesses, which met for the first time in 1619. In its charter, the Virginia Company had been given the responsibility of running its settlements in Virginia by appointing governors and other officers.

The stockholders of the Virginia Company considered themselves to be like a parliament for the young community, but from the beginning they worried about dictating how the colonists should live and were reluctant to levy taxes "without their consent first."[10] They knew that they would have little control if the colonists disagreed with their decisions. Thus, the Virginia Company directed the colonists to assemble a group of settlers to help make decisions.

In one colony after another, representative assemblies emerged from the need for order. Once in place, these assemblies were impossible to ignore or uproot. When Virginia became a royal colony in 1624, with a governor appointed by the king, the House of Burgesses insisted that the governor "shall not lay any taxes or impositions upon the colony, their lands or commodities otherwise than by the authority of the General Assembly, to be levied and employed" as it directed.[11]

By the early 1700s, all thirteen colonies had given their representative assemblies

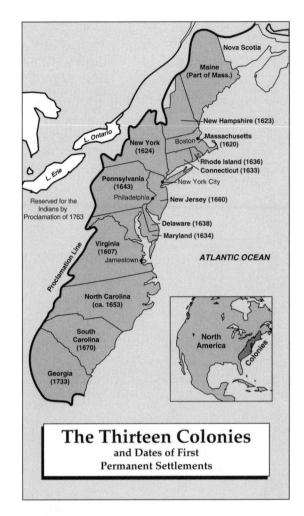

The Thirteen Colonies
and Dates of First
Permanent Settlements

the power to govern community affairs, levy taxes, and appropriate funds. Each of the colonies also had a governor who served as the main representative to England. In most of the colonies, the governor was appointed by the king, and the governors usually considered England, rather than the colonies, their home.

The colonies' charters gave the governors broad powers. They could summon or dismiss the elected assemblies, veto legislation, and appoint officials. In most colonies, the governor appointed a council, which not only served as the upper house of the legislature but as the colony's highest court. However, the governors' powers were far stronger on paper than in reality. Dependent on the elected assemblies for funds—often including their own salaries—the colonial governors could little afford to antagonize the colonists.

THE RIGHTS OF ENGLISHMEN

According to the charters governing the English colonies, the colonists in America were guaranteed the same rights and freedoms as those who lived in England. Some of these rights were delineated in the Magna Carta, which had been drafted in

---

CONNECTICUT RESOLVES OF 1639

As people came together in villages and towns, they needed a way to govern their own behavior. In its "Fundamental Orders of 1639," Connecticut outlined such issues as how members of the elected assemblies would be elected and how often they would meet. This excerpt is from The Federal and State Constitutions, Colonial Charters, and Other Organic Laws of the States, Territories, and Colonies Now or Heretofore Forming the United States of America, *compiled and edited by Francis Newton Thorpe.*

"For as much as it hath pleased Almighty God by the wise disposition of his divine providence so to order and dispose of things that we the Inhabitants and Residents of Windsor, Hartford and Wethersfield are now cohabiting and dwelling in and upon the River of Connectecotte [Connecticut] and the lands thereunto adjoining; and well knowing where a people are gathered together the word of God requires that to maintain the peace and union of such a people there should be an orderly and decent Government established according to God, to order and dispose of the affairs of the people at all seasons as occasion shall require; do therefore associate and conjoin ourselves to be as one Public State or Commonwealth; and do for ourselves and our successors and such as shall be adjoined to us at any time hereafter, enter into Combination and Confederation together, to maintain and preserve the liberty and purity of the Gospel of our Lord Jesus which we now profess, as also, the discipline of the Churches, which according to the truth of the said Gospel is now practiced amongst us; as also in our civil affairs to be guided and governed according to such Laws, Rules, Orders and Decrees as shall be made, ordered, and decreed."

1215. This "Great Charter" listed rights that landowners and church leaders demanded from the English monarch. In 1689, Parliament set forth additional liberties in a Declaration of Rights. The declaration affirmed freedom of speech and the right to a jury trial. It also guaranteed that no British subjects could be taxed without their consent, given through their elected representatives in Parliament. This set the stage for the famous rallying cry during the American colonists' struggle for freedom: "No taxation without representation!"

In addition, in one colony after another, bills of rights were incorporated into colonial laws and constitutions. The Massachusetts Body of Liberties of 1641, which guaranteed freedom of speech, the right to petition the colonial government, and trial by jury, became a model for similar legislation in other colonies. The Maryland Act of the Liberties of the People declared that "all the inhabitants of this Province being Christians (slaves excepted) should have such rights, liberties, immunities, privileges, and free customs"[12] of English citizens. Protection for these "unalienable rights" was a main reason for the movement for independence in the American colonies. The various bills of rights also served as the basis of the U.S. Bill of Rights, which makes up the first ten amendments of the U.S. Constitution.

MERCANTILISM

As the colonists focused their energies on internal affairs, England set up an interdependent trade relationship with her

England's King John signing the Magna Carta.

colonies that became known as mercantilism. In exchange for raw goods from her colonies, England traded the manufactured goods that Americans needed. The mercantile system was based on the theory that England could become strong by regulating trade to favor British industry.

When first founded, the colonies had engaged in profitable trade with a number of partners—Holland, France, and Spain, as well as other colonies—but it was not long before England passed laws to restrict the rights of colonists to trade freely. Early laws had listed only a few items which had to be brought directly from England, but over time the list grew longer and longer. The strictest elements of the mercantilism policy were the Navigation Acts, which originally promoted the use of ships manufactured, owned, and manned by citizens of England or the colonies. By 1696, increasingly more rigid Navigation Acts required that all European goods for the colonies must come from England or pass through an English port. In addition, the colonies were required to trade most items only with England, and all trade between the colonies and England had to be conducted on ships built, owned, and piloted by Englishmen or English colonists.

Generally, both England and her colonies benefited from mercantilism. Trade with England provided the colonies with a steady trade partner and a steady income. For the most part, the colonists saw the Navigation Acts mainly as an inconvenience. Although they were strict, they were not easily enforced. The most troubling of the laws was the restriction on trade with the French West Indies—a law that the colonists learned to avoid through smuggling.

SEEDS OF INDEPENDENCE

Although the colonists were basically content with their relations with England, the seeds of independence had been planted on American soil. The physical and emotional distance between the colonies and their mother country contributed to an independent, self-reliant spirit. By the mid-1700s, the colonies were fiercely defiant about their right to govern community affairs without outside interference. Increasingly, there was little to remind them of their connection to England. Apart from the royal governors, the only officials from the British govern-

ment who were involved in colonial affairs were the people charged with enforcing the Navigation Acts. But the colonists had learned how to live with most of the Navigation Acts and avoid those that were a nuisance. Thus, the average colonist might go through years, or even a lifetime, without seeing an officer of the British Empire.

The physical distance between England and her colonies made government difficult. England was dependent on mail for news about her colonies, but the mail service was slow and unreliable. Sometimes several months—or even years—would go by without correspondence between individual colonies and the mother country. A regular monthly mail boat between England and the American colonies was finally established in 1755. "By then it was too late," writes historian Daniel Boorstin. "In the American colonies there had already grown up thirteen separate centers of government. Self-government had come to stay, simply from force of circumstance—from the force of three thousand miles of ocean. If Americans wanted to be well governed, they had to govern themselves."[13]

DIVERSITY IN THE COLONIES

Between 1700 and 1760, the thirteen colonies grew sixfold in size. Although all the colonists were under British rule, the number of colonists who had been born and raised in America increased each year; a growing number had never set foot on English soil. The pattern of immigration also was changing; more and more people were coming from countries other than England. By the mid-1700s, almost a quarter of the population consisted of Germans and Scotch-Irish.

Each colony had different customs, religions, and economic interests. Especially pronounced were the differences between the northern colonies, which depended on manufacturing and trade, and the southern colonies, which depended on slavery to work tobacco and rice plantations. As the colonies received more and more immigrants from various countries, they became increasingly diverse in ethnicity and religion. By the middle of the eighteenth century, Massachusetts, Rhode Island, and Connecticut were the only states whose residents were still primarily of English heritage.

The colonists of 1760 were far more likely than those of the previous generation to consider themselves citizens of their colony first, and of England second. The growing ethnic, cultural, and religious diversity meant that there were fewer colonists who felt allegiance to the British Crown. In addition, the Scotch-Irish immigrants had already had bitter experiences with British rule before they arrived in America. America's practice of slavery separated her further from England. By 1750, almost an eighth of the colonial population consisted of African slaves.

The immigration experience may have contributed to the American Revolution in yet another way. Some people believe that the independent and willful spirit of the colonists was a product of that immigration experience. Arthur Young, an agricultural writer who lived in the colonies, noted, "Men who emigrate are, from the nature of

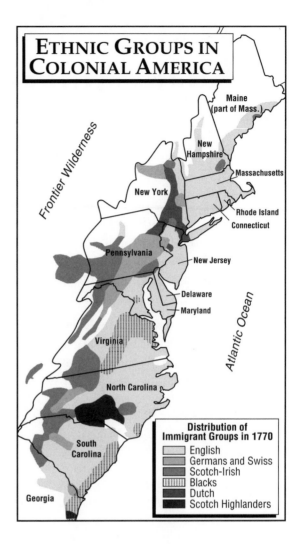

ETHNIC GROUPS IN COLONIAL AMERICA

Maine (part of Mass.)
New Hampshire
Massachusetts
New York
Rhode Island
Connecticut
Pennsylvania
New Jersey
Delaware
Maryland
Virginia
North Carolina
South Carolina
Georgia
Frontier Wilderness
Atlantic Ocean

Distribution of Immigrant Groups in 1770
- English
- Germans and Swiss
- Scotch-Irish
- Blacks
- Dutch
- Scotch Highlanders

the circumstances, the most active, hardy, daring, bold and resolute spirits, and probably the most mischievous also."[14] This resolute spirit contributed to a growing indignation at the way the colonies were treated by the mother country.

While the colonists were willing to live under England's rules as long as they benefited from them, it would not be long before they defiantly protested decisions that were in direct conflict with their own, uniquely American, interests.

2 The American Spirit

The American Revolution was more than a war—it was a revolution in thought that began long before the first shot was fired. Looking back on the revolutionary experience, John Adams asked in 1815,

> What do we mean by the Revolution? The war? That was no part of the Revolution; it was only an effect and consequence of it. The Revolution was in the minds of the people, and this was effected, from 1760 to 1775, in the course of fifteen years before a drop of blood was shed at Lexington.[15]

This revolution in thinking formed the cornerstone of the Constitution of the United States. From 1760 to 1775, Americans ceased to consider themselves subjects of England, governed by a king and Parliament four thousand miles away. As they gave voice to their complaints with England, a new consciousness slowly emerged—a uniquely American way of thinking. Among the fundamental principles of this new consciousness was the right to self-government and protection from tyranny. And, the colonists had come to believe that the best way to guard against tyranny was through a written constitution.

COLONIAL RIVALRIES

Before the mid-1700s, the colonies were completely independent of one another. There were no governmental or political entities that developed policy for the colonies as a whole. Such intercolonial groups were created only in response to the major events of the next several decades—the French and Indian War and then the struggle for independence.

The colonies bickered over the boundaries between them. They also argued over currency, trade, and religion. The colonies even failed to help one another defend against Indian attacks.

Even within the colonies themselves intense rivalries existed. Residents of rural areas often were suspect of the cities. James Otis, a Massachusetts lawyer who became a leader in the struggle against Britain, predicted in 1765 that "were the colonies left to themselves tomorrow, America would be a mere shambles of blood and confusion."[16]

A decade before the Declaration of Independence, union among the colonies seemed highly improbable, if not impossible. "We never can be made an independent people except it be by Great Britain

A New American

In the mid–eighteenth century, a growing number of Americans had no ties to England or loyalty to the king. A uniquely American character was developing. What was this American like? Michel Guillaume Jean de Crevecoeur, an immigrant from France, wrote Letters from an American Farmer, *an idealized vision of American colonial life in the 1760s. In the following excerpt from Page Smith's* A New Age Now Begins, *Crevecoeur argues that the American is different from his English counterparts.*

"What then is the American, this new man?

He is an American, who leaving behind him all his ancient prejudices and manners, receives new ones from the new mode of life he has embraced, the new government he obeys, and the new rank he holds. He becomes an American by being received in the broad lap of our great Alma Mater. Here the individuals of all nations are melted into a new race of men, whose labours and posterity will one day cause great changes in the world. . . . The American is a new man, who acts upon new principles; he must therefore entertain new ideas, and form new opinions. From involuntary idleness, servile dependence, penury, and useless labour, he has passed to toils of a very different sort, rewarded by ample subsistence. This is an American. . . .

American society is not composed, as in Europe, of great lords who possess every thing, and a herd of people who have nothing. . . . The rich and the poor are not so far removed from each other as they are in Europe. . . . We are a people of cultivators, scattered over an immense territory . . . united by silken cords of mild government, all respecting the laws, without dreading their power, because they are equitable."

herself," wrote John Dickinson, a Pennsylvania farmer, lawyer, and statesman, in a 1765 letter, "and the only way for her to do it is to make us frugal, ingenious, united, and discontented."[17]

The Albany Plan

England and France were fierce competitors in the New World. Each rushed to stake its claim to land and to gain an advantage in trade and commerce. In 1754, competing claims over the Ohio Valley touched off war. The French had laid claim to this territory, and its trade relationship with the Native Americans had proved profitable.

In June 1754, just weeks before the armed conflict began, representatives from the colonies met with 150 Iroquois leaders in Albany, New York, in an attempt to build an alliance with the powerful Iroquois Confederacy, a group of several Native American nations. The colonial delegates also discussed how they might be able to work together to forestall the impending war. Benjamin Franklin, the representative from Pennsylvania, proposed that the colonies join together, utilizing a common representative council elected by the colonial legislatures and a governor-general appointed by the Crown. The council would assume responsibility for the western affairs of all the colonies—for trade, Native American policy, and defense.

The colonial assemblies rejected the plan. They saw no need to diminish their independence or to forge relationships with one another. Later, Franklin said that his plan would have helped England and her colonies avoid war with one another. He felt that the plan

> would have been happy for both Sides. . . . The Colonies so united would have been sufficiently strong to have defended themselves; there would then have been no need of Troops from England; of course the subsequent Pretence for Taxing America, and the bloody Contest it occasioned, would have been avoided. But such Mistakes are not new; History is full of the Errors of States & Princes.[18]

THE FRENCH AND INDIAN WAR

The controversy in the Ohio Valley touched off a seven-year war with France. As British subjects, the American colonists were recruited to fight with the English.

Although Benjamin Franklin's suggestions that the colonies unite to defend themselves against the French was not implemented, his views eventually helped shape the future of America.

Ironically, rather than bringing them closer together, the war served to heighten tension between England and her colonists.

The colonial assemblies resisted providing money and men for the war waged by England. This angered England greatly. The English felt that the war was fought to defend colonists from French aggression and protect their trade rights, so the colonies should bear a large portion of its cost. England was further outraged that the colonists continued to trade with the Spanish and French West Indies during the war. England saw this as nothing short of aiding and abetting the enemy.

The colonists, on their part, became increasingly resentful of the British troops. The British treated the colonial militiamen not as equals but as inferiors. Under the military system in place, British officers commanded colonial troops, but colonial officers were not allowed to command English soldiers. The colonial assemblies began to argue with England over control of the colonial militia. Civilians, too, began to resent the presence of British troops in their midst.

WAR'S AFTERMATH

After seven long years of conflict, France surrendered. In the peace treaty, France ceded to England territory in what is now Canada; Spain, France's ally, ceded present-day Florida.

The war had a profound impact on Britain's relationship with her colonies. After years of statutory neglect during which England had allowed the American colonies to basically rule themselves, Britain had come to the opinion that

tighter control was needed. Two measures were passed almost immediately. England forbade European settlement west of the Appalachian Mountains, hoping to avoid the expense of war with Native Americans, and prohibited colonial assemblies from using paper money to pay off debts. Instead, they would have to use gold. This measure was intended to deal with the skyrocketing inflation that occurred because some of the colonies had attempted to pay off their war debts by issuing more paper money.

Although the war had ended, England left behind troops in America, ostensibly to protect the colonists from further aggression by the wartime enemies. However, the colonists suspected a different motive. They believed that England intended to use the troops to control them. Their resentment grew when they were expected to continue to provide the troops with housing and to pay for their upkeep.

The French and Indian War raised tensions between England and the colonists.

PARLIAMENT TAXES THE COLONIES

The French and Indian War had been expensive. Parliament searched for ways to generate money in the American colonies to pay off what George Grenville, England's prime minister, called "an expence arising from themselves."[19] In 1764, Parliament passed the Sugar Act, which levied a tax on the import of this commodity. The colonists knew the power of taxation. Parliament's exclusive power to tax—a power denied to the king—was an important guarantee of rights in English law. Some colonists wanted to issue a prompt denial of Parliament's authority to tax them. The New York assembly sent a petition outlining its case:

> An Exemption from the Burthen of ungranted, involuntary Taxes, must be the grand Principle of every free State. Without such a Right vested in themselves, exclusive of all others, there can be no Liberty, no Happiness, no Security; it is inseparable from the very idea of Property, for who can call that his own, which may be taken away at the Pleasure of another?[20]

But the Sugar Act was more than just a tax. It also expanded the list of products that could be exported by the colonies only to England and made smuggling more difficult. Furthermore, the legislation took away any smuggler's right to a jury trial, giving British-appointed judges the power to decide all cases in which the tax was not paid.

Parliament was unconcerned about colonial reaction and just a year later passed the Stamp Act. This legislation re-

Revenue stamps were required to be placed on all paper products purchased by the colonists, indicating that a tax had been paid to Britain.

quired colonists to buy and place revenue stamps on legal documents, newspapers, pamphlets, playing cards, and other items. It also raised the level of debate in the American colonies. John Adams wrote in his diary that the legislation

> has raised and spread through the whole continent a spirit that will be recorded to our honor with all future generations. The people, even to the lowest ranks, have become more attentive to their liberties and more determined to defend them than they were ever known to be. Our presses have groaned, our pulpits have thundered, our legislatures have resolved, our towns have voted.[21]

THE STAMP ACT CONGRESS

In June 1765, Massachusetts called for a meeting to consider how to stop the taxes. In October, the colonies responded, convening the first intercolonial assembly, called the Stamp Act Congress, in New York. Nine of the thirteen colonies were represented; the remaining four sent word that they would agree to whatever was decided.

At the Stamp Act Congress, the colonial representatives resolved:

> That it is inseparably essential to the freedom of a people, and the undoubted right of Englishmen, that no taxes be imposed on them, but with their own consent, given personally, or by their representatives. That the people of these colonies are not, and from their local circumstances cannot be, represented in the House of Commons in Great-Britain. That the only representatives of the people of these colonies, are persons chosen therein by themselves, and that no taxes ever have been, or can be constitutionally imposed on them, but by their respective legislatures.[22]

The congress further asserted that the British Stamp Act denied the colonists fundamental rights as Englishmen, including the rights to petition the Crown and trial by jury. Finally, it said that the taxes were "burdenson and grievous, . . . the payment of them [was] absolutely impracticable."[23]

The colonists agreed to boycott the Stamp Act. They refused to use the stamps and circulated unstamped newspapers and pamphlets. Violence erupted in several cities when colonists clashed with stamp collectors, but the boycott succeeded. Just three months after its passage, Parliament repealed the Stamp Act.

An early political cartoon depicts the people of Boston tarring and feathering a tax collector.

A CLASH OF PRINCIPLES

If the colonists celebrated, they did so too soon. The American colonists' position that England had no right to tax them fell on deaf ears. Just after it repealed the Stamp Act, Parliament passed the Declaratory Act, which asserted that parliament had "full power and authority to make laws and statutes of sufficient force and validity to bind the colonies and the people of America in all cases whatsoever."[24]

Underlying the conflict between England and her colonies was a fundamental difference in their beliefs about representative government. The English system of government was predicated on the belief that Parliament represented all citizens of the British Empire—in all her colonies throughout the world. But the American colonies had given birth to a tradition of popularly elected assemblies in which each county elected its own representatives to represent the interests of a specific area. In the colonists' opinion, they had no "virtual representation" in Parliament.

England believed that the opposition to the Stamp Act was based on the principle that Parliament had no right to impose *internal* taxes, but allowing Britain the right to pass *external* taxes. This was a misunderstanding of the resolute determination on the part of the Americans to oppose all taxation measures passed without their consent.

THE TOWNSHEND ACTS

Charles Townshend, the British chancellor of the Exchequer, believed that the repeal of the Stamp Acts was cowardly and that Parliament had been unwise to give in to the seditious spirit of the colonies. In 1767, he proposed a series of legislation that would strengthen the power of the Crown in the colonies and raise the necessary funds to support Britain's presence. The first such act called for the suspension of the New York assembly in punishment for refusing to comply with the Quartering Act, which required New Yorkers to pay for the upkeep of British troops in the colony. The second measure, the Revenue Act, imposed duties on the import of glass, lead, paints, paper, and tea—all of which could be purchased only from England according to the Navigation Act still in effect. To make enforcement easier, the Revenue Act gave extensive power to a new board of customs commissioners and made general search warrants legal.

The colonial response to the Townshend Acts was immediate. A torrent of newspaper editorials, pamphlets, and other documents proclaimed that Parliament was trampling the colonists' rights. Among these were "Letters from a Farmer in Pennsylvania," written by John Dickinson, which carefully examined and dissected the powers of Parliament and the limitations on these powers. In one letter he wrote,

> Parliament unquestionably possesses a legal authority to regulate the trade of Great Britain and all her colonies. . . . Such an authority is . . . necessary for the common good of all. [But] if you ONCE admit that Great Britain may lay duties upon her exportations to us, *for the purpose of levying money on us only* she will have nothing to do but to lay those duties on the articles which she prohibits us to manufacture—and the tragedy of American liberty is finished.[25]

The colonies believed that economic pressure was their best weapon and agreed to boycott the taxed items. By early 1769, all thirteen colonies had in place nonimportation agreements. The colonists were also becoming better organized. At the suggestion of Samuel Adams, a Boston patriot, the Massachusetts assembly established a formal committee charged with sharing information about Britain's attacks on colonial liberties. Other colonial assemblies soon followed suit. These Committees of Correspondence formed a core of patriots who were prepared to work together to document further violations of colonial rights.

The Townshend Acts had accomplished what the French and Indian War had not: It

LETTERS FROM A PENNSYLVANIA FARMER

John Dickinson, who would later draft the Articles of Confederation and serve as a delegate at the Constitutional Convention, wrote a series of letters capturing the essence of the colonies' complaints about Parliament's power. In the twelfth and last letter, excerpted here from Page Smith's A New Age Now Begins, *Dickinson cautions England against pushing the colonists too far.*

"Let these truths be indelibly impressed on our minds— that we cannot be happy without being free—that we cannot be free without being secure in our property—that we cannot be secure in our property if without our consent others may as by right take it away—that taxes imposed on us by Parliament do thus take it away—that duties laid for the sole purpose of raising money are taxes—that attempts to lay such duties should be instantly and firmly opposed—that this opposition can never be effectual unless it is the united effort of these Provinces—that therefore benevolence of temper towards each other and unanimity of councils are essential to the welfare of the whole—and lastly, that for this reason, every man amongst us who in any manner would encourage either dissension, diffidence, or indifference between these colonies is an enemy to himself and to his country."

John Dickinson spoke movingly about the importance of liberty.

forged an alliance among the colonies. Inter-colonial cooperation and communication would be key to their victory in the upcoming struggle with England.

The Townshend Acts proved ineffective as well as unpopular. Taxes on Britain's exports to the colonies were not favorable to British trade and brought in little revenue. Parliament considered repealing the measures but did not want to appear to be backing down because of American resistance. In 1770, British leaders decided the best solution was to repeal all the measures except one: a tax on tea.

THE BOSTON TEA PARTY

With the repeal of the Townshend Acts, the colonies entered a period of relative stability. However, the simple commodity of tea would once again heighten the revolutionary spirit in America.

The trouble began when Parliament passed the Tea Act in May 1773. Although this piece of legislation in fact lowered the tax on tea, it also allowed the British East India Company to distribute tea directly to colonial retailers, bypassing American colonial merchants. Thus, the East India Company could undercut the price of the Dutch tea being smuggled into the colonies.

The colonists saw the Tea Act as a way to trick them into paying a tax on tea. They wanted no part of the East India Company tea, no matter how cheaply it came. New York and Philadelphia sent the ships carrying tea back to England, but the royal governor of Massachusetts refused to allow the ships in Boston Harbor to leave the port. The colonists were adamant about not allowing the tea to be sold in America. On December 16, a group of men disguised as Mohawk Indians stole onto the tea ships and dumped forty-five tons of tea overboard.

Colonists disguised as Mohawk Indians dump tea into Boston Harbor in protest of England's attempts to control them.

Unlike earlier defiant gestures, the Boston Tea Party was a well-planned, premeditated act of rebellion. As historian Page Smith explains,

> By now the patriot leaders had established firm control. There were no rioters among the carefully drilled Mohawks who dumped the tea in Boston Harbor; they were rather a corps of irregulars who might, on the next occasion, carry loaded muskets. But if they did so it would be in response to orders, not to the volatile passions of a mob.[26]

PARLIAMENT UPS THE ANTE

England refused to consider retreat or compromise. Instead, Parliament passed measures intended to isolate the radical element in Massachusetts and to intimidate the more moderate colonies into obedience.

Parliament demanded compensation for the lost tea and closed the port of Boston until the debt was paid. It then passed legislation that curtailed the powers of the colonial representative assembly, granting broad new powers to the royal governor, and stripped the right of the representative assembly to elect the governor's council. Massachusetts government officials who were charged with a crime would be tried in England.

The colonists were outraged by these measures, which they labeled the "Intolerable Acts." People in other colonies did not turn away from Massachusetts as Britain had hoped. Rather, they pledged to join in defense of Massachusetts and any other colony stripped of its rights.

THE FIRST CONTINENTAL CONGRESS

In September 1774, fifty-five delegates from twelve of the thirteen colonies met at the First Continental Congress in Philadelphia. They declared the Intolerable Acts to be unconstitutional, and reiterated that Parliament had no power to tax the colonists without their consent. They resolved to boycott all trade with England—exports as well as imports. The boycott would remain in effect until England had addressed all grievances. To work together toward this end, the colonies formed a Continental Association, which included the original Committees of Correspondence.

The discussions that took place at the First Continental Congress reveal how far the colonies had come. For the first time, the colonists began to see their common interests rather than their differences. "The distinctions between Virginians, Pennsylvanians, New Yorkers, and New Englanders are no more," announced Patrick Henry in a speech before Congress. "I am not a Virginian but an American."[27] The colonists were beginning to form a national identity, an identity nourished by stalwart resistance to British tyranny.

THE SHOT HEARD 'ROUND THE WORLD

The colonists got ready to put muscle behind their words. They formed local militia units and stockpiled arms and ammunition. In Massachusetts, which had become the hotbed of hostilities, local residents were trained to be up and ready at a moment's notice. Thus, they became known as Minutemen.

In April 1775, when British troops headed to Concord, Massachusetts, to seize the colonists' weapons, the Minutemen were ready. Forewarned by Paul Revere in his famous ride, about seventy men were gathered on the town green when the British troops marched into Lexington. But they were far outnumbered by the British. Just as they began to disperse, a shot rang out. It was never established who fired that "shot heard 'round the world," but it was followed by a barrage of bullets. Within minutes, eight Americans lay dead and another ten wounded. These were the first casualties of the American Revolution.

The British continued their march on to Concord. American colonists were not going to let them go easily, however. They harassed them at every turn, firing from behind trees and buildings. When the British reached Concord, the colonists converged on a small platoon and forced them to turn back. The colonial militiamen continued to plague the British troops all the way back to Boston. When the conflict was over, British casualties numbered more than 270, American casualties fewer than 100. The colonists hailed this as a victory. It proved to both sides that the colonial militia was both willing and able to fight.

COMMON SENSE

As the first shots of the Revolutionary War were exchanged, a revolution was taking place in hearts and minds as well. The colonists were growing increasingly con-

Paul Revere makes his famous ride.

THE REVOLUTIONARY SPIRIT

By the mid-1770s, newspapers openly discussed the advantages of independence. This poem by Philip Freneau, reprinted from Page Smith's A New Age Now Begins, *exemplifies the revolutionary spirit that had taken hold of the colonies.*

Too long our patient country wears her chains,
Too long our wealth all-grasping Britain drains:
Why still a handmaid to that distant land?
Why still subservient to their proud command?
Fallen on disastrous times, they scorn our plea:
'Tis our own efforts that must make us free. . . .

From the scoundrel, Lord North, who would bind
  us in chains.
From a dunce of a king who was born without brains.
From an island that bullies, and hectors, and swears.
I send up to heaven my wishes and prayers
That we, disunited, may freemen be still,
And Britain go on—to be damned, If she will.

vinced that a break with England was the only way they could escape from the crushing taxes and Parliament's bullying. Newspaper editorials, broadsides, and brochures lambasted the British and called for independence.

Among the most popular publications during this time was *Common Sense,* a fifty-page pamphlet written by Thomas Paine. Unlike many of the political treatises on which the ideas behind the Revolution were based, *Common Sense* was written for the common man. It gave voice to the complaints of the American colonists and attacked King George III and the British aristocracy. *Common Sense* went beyond criticizing the current British regime, however. It urged the colonists to take action. Paine argued that the American colonies had a moral obligation to become an independent nation, with power to govern in the hands of citizens and their elected representatives:

Every thing that is right or reasonable pleads for separation. The blood of the slain, the weeping voice of nature cries, 'Tis time to part. Even the distance at which the Almighty hath placed England and America, is a strong and natural proof, that the authority of the one, over the other, was never the design of Heaven. . . . To be always running three or four thousand miles with a tale or a petition, waiting four or five months for an answer, which, when obtained, requires five or six more to explain it in, will in a few years be looked upon as folly

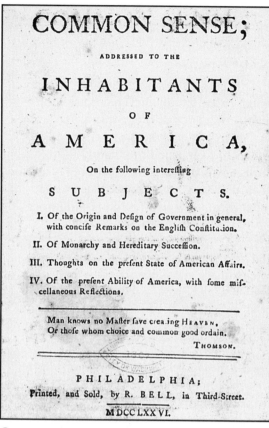

COMMON SENSE;

ADDRESSED TO THE

INHABITANTS

OF

AMERICA,

On the following interesting

SUBJECTS.

I. Of the Origin and Design of Government in general,
with concise Remarks on the English Constitution.

II. Of Monarchy and Hereditary Succession.

III. Thoughts on the present State of American Affairs.

IV. Of the present Ability of America, with some mis-
cellaneous Reflections.

Man knows no Master save creating HEAVEN,
Or those whom choice and common good ordain.
THOMSON.

PHILADELPHIA;

Printed, and Sold, by R. BELL, in Third-Street.

MDCCLXXVI.

Common Sense, a pamphlet written by Thomas Paine, encouraged the colonists to break with Britain and form an independent nation.

and childishness. There was a time when it was proper, and there is a proper time for it to cease.[28]

Common Sense quickly became the most widely read document of its time. About 150,000 copies were bought in just six months, and copies were passed from one person to the next, so that more than 1 million Americans—about half the population—read it. Historian Page Smith even suggests that "To say that it [*Common Sense*] was the most successful political pamphlet in history

is to do it insufficient credit. *Common Sense* belongs in a category all its own."[29]

As the popularity of *Common Sense* indicates, the idea of self-government had taken hold in the colonies. The colonists wanted a government that would be responsive to their needs and economic interests. They wanted a clear voice in governmental decisions. They longed for protection from tyranny and relief from empty promises. Their ideals were encapsulated in the Declaration of Independence. Later, these ideals would serve as the principles underlying the new constitution.

THE CONTINENTAL CONGRESS VOTES FOR INDEPENDENCE

With public sentiment increasingly in favor of independence, the colonial assemblies began to speak of independence in earnest. In June 1776, Richard Henry Lee, a renowned planter and delegate from Virginia, read a resolution before the Continental Congress:

> RESOLVED: That these United Colonies are, and of right ought to be, free and independent States, that they are absolved from all allegiance to the British Crown, and that all political connection between them and the State of Great Britain is, and ought to be, totally dissolved.[30]

After much debate, twelve of the thirteen colonies voted for Lee's resolution. (New York, which had a large population of Loyalists, who favored staying with England, abstained.) Congress appointed

COMMON SENSE

In the midst of pre-revolutionary fervor, Thomas Paine, a recent immigrant from England, published a fifty-page pamphlet that touched the hearts and souls of the common person. Common Sense *asserted that the American colonies were being exploited by Great Britain and that they received no advantage from keeping their ties to the king. In the following excerpts, taken from Paine's* Collected Writings, *he calls upon his fellow Americans to stand up and fight.*

"Every thing that is right or reasonable pleads for separation. The blood of the slain, the weeping voice of nature cries, 'Tis time to part. Even the distance at which the Almighty hath placed England and America, is a strong and natural proof, that the authority of the one, over the other, was never the design of Heaven. . . . It is repugnant to reason, to the universal order of things, to all examples from former ages, to suppose that this continent can long remain subject to any external power. . . . The utmost stretch of human wisdom cannot, at this time, compass a plan, short of separation, which can promise the continent even a year's security. . . .

To be always running three or four thousand miles with a tale or a petition, waiting four or five months for an answer, which, when obtained, requires five or six more to explain it in, will in a few years be looked upon as folly and childishness. There was a time when it was proper, and there is a proper time for it to cease. . . .

A government of our own is our natural right: And when a man seriously reflects on the precariousness of human affairs, he will become convinced, that it is infinitely wiser and safer, to form a constitution of our own in a cool deliberate manner, while we have it in our power, than to trust such an interesting event to time and chance.

The last cord is now broken. . . .There are injuries which nature cannot forgive. O ye that love mankind! Ye that dare oppose not only the tyranny but the tyrant, stand forth! Every spot of the old world is overrun with oppression. Freedom hath been hunted round the globe. . . . O! receive the fugitive and prepare in time an asylum for mankind."

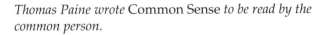

Thomas Paine wrote Common Sense *to be read by the common person.*

a committee to prepare a document justifying freedom and explaining the reasons for choosing to break with England. Thomas Jefferson, a young lawyer from Virginia, was chosen to prepare the first draft. In Jefferson's words, the document was intended "to place before mankind the common sense of the subject, in terms so plain and firm as to command their assent."

In the Declaration of Independence, Jefferson asserted that the main purpose of government is to protect the rights of "life, liberty, and the pursuit of happiness." All human beings possess certain inalienable rights that no government could take away.

Furthermore, government derives its power from the consent of the governed. Because England had not governed justly, the people no longer consented to be governed by England. The Declaration of Independence thus claimed the right of the colonies to be independent.

The ideas in the Declaration of Independence seem commonplace today, but they were radical in the eighteenth century. As one historian explains, "It was not self-evident in 1776 that all men are created equal, that governments derive their authority from popular consent, or that good governments exist in order to protect God-given rights."[31]

Members of the Second Continental Congress gather for the signing of the Declaration of Independence.

KING GEORGE ON THE DECLARATION OF INDEPENDENCE

King George III considered the Declaration of Independence a desperate act of a few rebel leaders that threatened not only the safety of his colonies, but the mercantile system. He made the following speech to the House of Lords on October 31, 1776. It is excerpted from Jim R. McClellan, Historical Moments: Changing Interpretations of America's Past.

"[S]o daring and desperate is the Spirit of those Leaders, whose Object has always been Domination and Power, that they have now openly renounced all Allegiance to the Crown: They have . . . presumed to set up their rebellious Confederacies for Independent States. If their Treason be suffered to take Root, much Mischief must grow from it, to the Safety of my loyal Colonies, to the Commerce of my Kingdoms, and indeed to the present System of all Europe. One great Advantage, however, will be derived from the Object of the Rebels being openly avowed and clearly understood; We shall have Unanimity at Home, founded in the general Conviction of the Justice and Necessity of our Measures."

King George III grossly misjudged the determination of most colonists to break with England.

THE NEED FOR A NEW GOVERNMENT

On July 4, 1776, the delegates at the Second Continental Congress signed the Declaration of Independence. With the stroke of a pen, the colonies claimed their right to be free. But the Declaration of Independence stopped short of describing how the new states would govern themselves. How would they work together? Who would make the decisions that would affect them all? How would leaders be selected?

The founding fathers realized that a new system of government was needed. They also recognized the need to forge alliances in order to defeat England. To this end, they resolved "to take the most effectual measures for forming foreign Alliances" and "that a plan of confederation be prepared and transmitted to the respective Colonies for their consideration and approbation."[32] These Articles of Confederation would become the nation's first attempt at self-government.

Chapter

3 An Attempt at Self-Government

When the Declaration of Independence was signed on July 4, 1776, the thirteen colonies proclaimed that they would no longer be governed by England. Now, they needed to develop a new system of government. Thus began one of the greatest experiments in political history.

The new American statesmen understood that they had a unique opportunity to fashion a government according to their principles. In 1777, John Jay, an esteemed New York lawyer who later became a leading advocate for the Constitution, wrote,

> The Americans are the first people whom Heaven has favoured with an opportunity of deliberating upon, and choosing, the forms of government under which they shall live. All other constitutions have derived their existence from violence or accidental circumstances, and are therefore probably more distant from their perfection, which, though beyond our reach, may nevertheless be approached under the guidance of reason and experience.[33]

When the founding fathers cut their ties with England, they destroyed the system under which they were governed. The colonial charters were no longer valid.

Recognizing the need to replace the colonial systems of government, American patriots began to craft new constitutions outlining government at the state level.

The founding fathers recognized that, in order to defeat the British, they needed some form of national government, but some states were reluctant to give up their own power to a national government. Thus, the first experiment—the Articles of Confederation—proved insufficient as a national government plan. However, both the state constitutions and the Articles of

Lawyer John Jay believed that independence from Britain gave colonists a unique opportunity to form a government based on their highest ideals.

Confederation proved to be important precursors to the U.S. Constitution.

THE STATES CLAIM SELF-GOVERNMENT

Between 1775 and 1780, all thirteen states put into place new systems of self-government. "This flurry of constitution-making was one of the most remarkable political episodes in history," writes historian Page Smith. "It demonstrated as nothing else could the degree of political sophistication that had developed in the American colonies in the years of crisis prior to the outbreak of hostilities."[34]

JOHN ADAMS PLANS FOR SELF-GOVERNMENT

Even before the Declaration of Independence, John Adams was planning for a new government. He was instrumental in encouraging the states to draft constitutions between 1776 and 1780. His sense of optimism is clear in this excerpt of a letter written in January 1776, taken from Winthrop D. Jordan's and Leon F. Littwack's The United States.

"As politics is the art of securing human happiness, and the prosperity of societies depends upon the constitution of government under which they live, there cannot be a more agreeable employment to a benevolent mind than the study of the best kinds of government.

It has been the will of Heaven that we should be thrown into existence at a period when the greatest philosophers and lawgivers of antiquity would have wished to live. A period when a coincidence of circumstances without example, has afforded to thirteen Colonies, at once, an opportunity of beginning government anew from the foundation, and building as they choose. How few of the human race have ever had any opportunity of choosing a system of government for themselves and their children! How few have ever had any thing more of choice in government than in climate! These Colonies have now their election; and it is much to be wished that it may not prove to be like a prize in the hands of a man who has no heart to improve it."

John Adams delighted in the idea of creating a government in which the people would have a say.

Virginia was the first state to complete a constitution. Virginia's constitution began with a bill of rights which asserted that all power was vested in the people. Other states quickly followed Virginia's example. Rhode Island and Connecticut adapted their charters by adding preambles and striking all references to the Crown of England; the eleven other states wrote new constitutions. By 1780, each of the thirteen states had a new government in place, outlined in a written document.

In writing the state constitutions, the colonists relied upon their experiences under British rule—both before and after hostilities broke out with the British. As one historian explains,

> The ex-colonists . . . still possessed an admiration for the British constitution that was only slightly tarnished by their recent experiences. . . . The problem was to design a government containing all the virtues of the British constitution but with added safeguards to prevent the kind of deterioration they had just witnessed.[35]

THE STATE CONSTITUTIONS

The state constitutions were based on the premise that they derived their legitimacy from the consent of those governed. Most had bicameral legislatures with broadened powers and an elected governor. Because the colonists' experience with royal governors made them cautious about vesting too much power in one person, the state constitutions granted only limited power to a chief executive. Pennsylvania's constitution gave the right to vote to all adult white males, but most of the other states continued to require the ownership of property as a condition for voting rights.

The new constitutions were not perfect, but they did protect more individual liberties than any previous governing document. To protect citizens against injustices that they had been exposed to under British rule, most had specific clauses that guaranteed traditional English legal rights, and some delineated these rights in a separate bill of rights. Rights commonly protected included religious freedom, trial by jury, and freedom of the press—all of which were incorporated into the U.S. Bill of Rights in 1789. The documents also reflected eighteenth-century Enlightenment values, guaranteeing religious freedom.

Not only were the state constitutions important self-governing documents, they were critical to the formation of the U.S. Constitution. "What is the Constitution of the United States," asserted John Adams in 1788, "but that of Massachusetts, New York and Maryland! There is not a feature in it which cannot be found in one or the other."[36] (An important exception is the Supreme Court.)

A LOOSE CONFEDERATION

Following the Declaration of Independence in 1776, the states voluntarily joined together in the Continental Congress. The Congress mediated disputes among the states, raised and maintained the Continental Army, and made alliances with France. However, this was a temporary government, without clearly defined powers. The representatives recognized the need for better delineating their authority.

In general, the citizens of the newly formed United States were fearful of a strong central government and wanted the states to be independent of one another. They wanted to protect the customs, religions, and social and economic structure that suited their particular state. The state constitutions protected the citizens' role in self-government—a role they were hesitant to give up. Since they were risking their lives to rid themselves of one powerful government, they were understandably hesitant to create another.

But Americans also recognized that England would be a tenacious foe. England had more experienced and better-equipped troops than the American militia. The states realized that they would need to work together to defeat her.

The leaders of the Continental Congress hit on a compromise solution with the Articles of Confederation. Drafted by John Dickinson of Pennsylvania, the Articles banded together the states in a "perpetual union" and a "firm league of friendship." They provided for a Congress, with representatives elected annually by the states. Congress was given the power to carry out the war against the British, manage foreign affairs, borrow and print money, and requisition funds from the states. The states would pay the salaries of their own representatives and would pay funds into a common treasury in proportion to the value of their land. Each state, regardless of its population,

had one vote on the issues brought before Congress. This would enable Congress to fund and carry out the war effort.

To accommodate the concerns of those who feared a strong central government, the Articles left intact the states' rights to govern their own affairs. Each state continued to write its own laws, issue its own paper money, and elect its own leaders.

REACTION TO THE PROPOSED ARTICLES

Not everyone agreed that this loose confederation of states was the best way to govern the states. Some people argued that stronger ties were needed to unify the states into an independent nation, strong enough to stand up to other nations. John Adams was among those who argued that the confederation would not have sufficient power to govern effectively. "Before 10 years this confederation, like a rope of sand, will be found inadequate to the purpose and its dissolution will take place," he wrote as the finishing touches were being put on the Articles. "Heaven grant that wisdom and experience may then avert what we have most to fear."[37]

Congress adopted the Articles in November 1777, but a number of the state legislatures refused to ratify them. They were wary of turning over power to a central political authority. Years after the Articles were proposed, the Continental Congress remained without formal authority to act. In 1780, General George Washington urged the states to ratify the Articles: "Circumstances conspire to show the necessity of immediately adopting a plan that will give more energy to Government. . . . Without it we have everything to fear."[38] In 1781, the last state, Maryland, voted for ratification, and the Articles took effect.

THE WAR EFFORT

In the meantime, the Revolutionary War expanded, and the Continental Congress struggled along without clear authority. The national government did not have power to levy taxes and faced the seemingly insurmountable obstacle of collecting the money owed by the states.

When George Washington took over the army in 1775, it consisted only of part-time militiamen dependent on their own arms and supplies. Washington called it "a mixed multitude of people . . . under very little discipline, order or government."[39] Although Washington managed to bring the army together under his command, equipping it as a modern militia proved beyond his capability.

The states were responsible for recruiting men for the army and were not always as diligent as Washington would have liked. Washington's main army never had more than twenty-four thousand active-duty troops, although Congress promised to raise a force at least three times that size. "The situation of our affairs at this period appears to me peculiarly critical," he wrote in a 1779 circular to state governments. "The state of the army in particular is alarming on several accounts, that of its numbers is not among the least."[40]

The majority of the recruits were without military experience. Often very young,

poor, and inexperienced, many signed up to receive a cash bonus and the promise of a future land grant. They often lacked discipline, and inadequate pay and poor requisitions contributed to the likelihood of mutiny or desertion.

General George Washington sent angry letters deploring the plight of his soldiers and begging the Continental Congress for money for ammunition, food, and clothing for his troops. On August 27, 1780, he sent an urgent dispatch:

George Washington takes command of the colonial army.

[T]he Army is again reduced to an extremity of distress for want of provision. The greater part of it had been without Meat from the 21st to the 26th. . . . We have not yet been absolutely without Flour, but we have this day but one day's supply in Camp. . . . [T]his army cannot possibly remain much longer together, unless very vigorous and immediate measures are taken by the States to comply with the requisitions made upon them. . . . Without a speedy change of circumstances, . . . either the Army must disband, or what is, if possible, worse, subsist upon the plunder of the people.[41]

THE TWO SIDES TAKE AIM

When fighting broke out in 1775, the British government believed it would be easy to crush the colonial revolt through military action. Britain had a large standing army, ample resources to employ additional troops, and the most powerful navy in the world.

The colonists, on the other hand, had an inexperienced and ill-equipped army. But it had one main advantage: The war was fought on American soil among a friendly population and familiar terrain. The American colonists also managed to forge alliances with France, Spain, and some of the Native American tribes and nations.

George Washington leads troops across the Delaware River on a surprise attack, defeating the larger, and better-prepared, troops in New York.

In the early struggle for New York, the British earned a decisive victory, as the mercenary Hessian troops it had employed pushed Washington and his troops across New Jersey and the Delaware River. Recognizing that he was overpowered militarily, Washington used the weapon of surprise. On December 25, 1776, he and about twenty-five hundred men recrossed the Delaware and surprised the Hessian troops as they slept, killing or wounding over a hundred and taking a thousand prisoners. Not a single American life was lost.

The next major campaign, the 1777 Battle of Saratoga, was also won by the colonists. British general John Burgoyne surrendered his entire army of fifty-seven hundred men. The Battle of Saratoga proved to be a critical turning point in the war. It boosted morale among the American troops, proving that they could succeed against the British. It also provided ammunition for Benjamin Franklin to convince France to enter the war in favor of the colonies. When news of Burgoyne's capture reached Paris in December 1777, France offered the Americans a commercial and military alliance.

THE WAR MOVES SOUTH

The British devised a new military strategy. They secured their northern bases of New York City and Newport, Rhode Island, concentrating their troops there. During the following year the Americans were able to capture only a few outlying fortresses, at Stony Point, New York, and Paulus Hook, New Jersey.

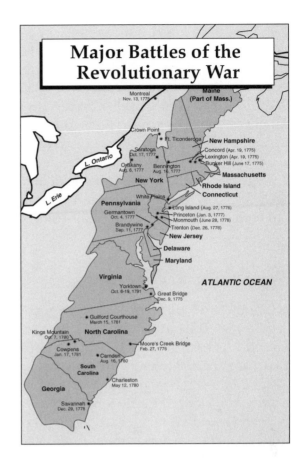

Major Battles of the Revolutionary War

This allowed the British to focus their efforts on subduing the South. They planned to use regular troops to capture territory and then to rely on local Loyalists to hold it. At first, they met with considerable success. An army of thirty-five hundred British troops captured Savannah, Georgia, at the end of December 1778, and within a year, had control over the entire state of Georgia. In May 1780, troops under the command of General Clinton took Charleston, capturing more than five thousand American troops.

However, Britain's southern strategy soon began to collapse. The colonists continued to wage guerrilla warfare against the British and Loyalist troops in Georgia and South Carolina and gradually cut the British lines of supply. At the same time, American troops and militia under the command of Nathanael Greene and "Light Horse" Harry Lee inflicted heavy casualties on the main British army. Even when the British regulars and Loyalists emerged victorious on the battlefield, they were forced to retreat because of American strength in the surrounding countryside.

SURRENDER IN YORKTOWN

General Cornwallis retreated to Virginia, where the British strategy finally collapsed. His troops began building a fortified base in Yorktown, Virginia. In July 1780, a French army of about five thousand men dislodged the British from Newport and threatened their garrison in New York City. The assistance from France gave Washington enough military force to launch a surprise attack on Cornwallis. The French navy positioned itself at the mouth of the Chesapeake River to prevent the supply or evacuation of Cornwallis's army. Meanwhile, Washington secretly moved troops to Virginia, where they joined an American army commanded by the Marquis de Lafayette, a French volunteer, and three thousand French troops. In all, this force comprised more than sixteen thousand. Recognizing that he was badly outnumbered, Cornwallis surrendered on October 19, 1781.

The French and American victory at Yorktown was even more devastating to the British cause than the earlier American triumph at Saratoga. After years of warfare, the British Parliament could not afford to continue. Although sporadic fighting persisted, England turned its attention to negotiating a peace treaty.

AN END TO THE REVOLUTION

After seven long years of fighting, the American Revolution ended with the Treaty of Paris, which was negotiated by Benjamin Franklin, in Paris; John Adams, in Holland; and John Jay, who was serving as the American foreign minister. The treaty was signed on September 3, 1783, and ratified in January 1784.

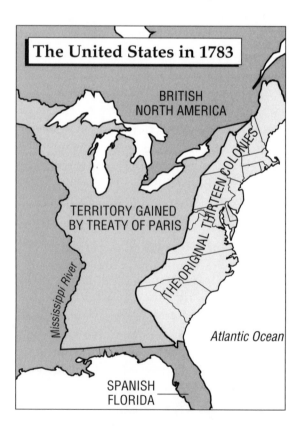

The United States in 1783

BRITISH NORTH AMERICA

TERRITORY GAINED BY TREATY OF PARIS

THE ORIGINAL THIRTEEN COLONIES

Mississippi River

Atlantic Ocean

SPANISH FLORIDA

In the treaty, England promised to withdraw her troop and conceded to the United States all the land between the Allegheny Mountains and the Mississippi River. The northern boundary ran to the Great Lakes, and the southern boundary was declared between Spanish Florida and Georgia on the 31st north latitude. In return, the United States promised to pay off all debts owed to England and pledged not to persecute those who had remained loyal to England.

With the Treaty of Paris, the United States was poised to operate as a free and independent nation. "Peace made, my dear friend, a new scene opens," wrote Alexander Hamilton, a New York lawyer who had served as an aide to George Washington, to his friend John Laurens. "The object will be to make our independence a blessing. To do this we must secure our Union on solid foundations. . . . It requires all the virtue and all the abilities of our country."[42] The new Americans felt the weight of their mission. South Carolina's Governor John Rutledge proclaimed, "The Eyes of Europe, nay of the World, are on America."[43]

DOMESTIC DISCORD AND DISPUTES

As America assumed its independence and looked toward the future, the Articles of Confederation helped the states make great strides forward. Not only had the war been won under this loose system of government, but the states were pleased with the terms of the peace treaty. The

Alexander Hamilton called for closer ties between states to develop a stronger nation.

confederation of states also signed the Northwest Ordinance, which established the process by which new states could enter the Union and dictated that all land north of the Ohio River would be "forever free" of slavery.

However, government under the Articles was trying. It had been difficult to get the states to agree on issues during the war; it became even more difficult after England was removed as a common enemy. The states soon began to bicker and to compete with one another. New York and New Hampshire fought over conflicting claims to Vermont; Maryland and Virginia argued over the navigation of the Potomac River.

The national government did not have the power to levy taxes and remained at the mercy of the state legislatures for funding. According to George Washington, congressional requisitions were "a perfect nullity where thirteen sovereign, independent, disunited states"[44] complied only when they chose to do so. In 1782, New Jersey was the only state to pay money to the national treasury, but even it gave a mere $5,500 of the $485,679 it owed. Robert Morris, Congress's treasurer, complained that the states "have been deaf to the calls of Congress, to the clamors of the public creditors, to the just demands of a suffering army, and even to the reproaches of the enemy, who scoffingly declare that the American Army is fed, paid, and clothed by France."[45]

The states that paid into the national treasury became increasingly bitter against those that did not. "New Hampshire has not paid a shilling since peace and does not ever mean to pay one to all eternity," complained a Virginian in 1787. "In New York," he added, "they pay well because they can do it by plundering New Jersey and Connecticut. Jersey will go to great lengths from motives of revenge and interest."[46] Trade between the states was hampered by a myriad of taxes. Some states levied taxes on any goods passing through their borders. "New Jersey," wrote Madison, "placed between Philadelphia and New York, was likened to a cask tapped at both ends; and North Carolina, between Virginia and South Carolina, to a patient bleeding at both arms."[47] Some states retained their own navies and negotiated their own trade agreements with other nations.

Social and political differences also contributed to friction among the states. By 1783, Rhode Island, Massachusetts, and Pennsylvania had made it illegal to own slaves; in New Jersey, freed black men were allowed to vote. Slaveholders in the South felt threatened by these developments and claimed the right to recapture any runaway slaves who fled to these states.

In 1787, James Wilson, a Pennsylvania lawyer who served several terms in the Continental Congress, described what had happened to the fledgling Union:

Among the first sentiments expressed in the first Congress one was that Virginia is no more, that Massachusetts is no more, that Pennsylvania is no more. We are now one nation of brethren. We must bury all local interests and distinctions. This language continued for some time. The tables at length began to turn. No sooner were the State Governments formed than their jealousy and ambition began to display themselves. Each endeavored to cut a slice from the common loaf, to add to its own morsel, till at length the confederation became frittered down to the impotent condition in which it now stands.[48]

WEAKNESSES IN THE ARTICLES

In September 1787, John Jay published a pamphlet that pointed out the problems associated with limiting the powers of Congress. According to Jay, under the Articles of Confederation, the members of Congress

may make war, but are not empowered to raise men or money to carry it on. They may make peace, but without ability to comply with the stipulations on their part—They may enter into treaties of commerce, but without power to enforce them at home or abroad—They may borrow money, but without having the means of repayment—They may partly regulate commerce, but without authority to execute their ordinances—They may appoint ministers and other officers of trust, but without power to try or punish them for misdemeanors—They may resolve, but cannot execute with dispatch or with secrecy—In short, they may consult, and deliberate, and recommend, and make requisitions, and they who please may regard them.[49]

Congress's inability to regulate trade made it difficult to direct the economy or address the postwar economic depression. Dependent on states to voluntarily contribute to the national government, Congress itself was constantly strapped for funds. It had tried to address this problem as early as 1782, when it proposed an amendment to the Articles of Confederation that would give the United States the right to levy a five percent duty on foreign imports. However, a unanimous vote of all the states was required to pass an amendment to the Articles, and Rhode Island rejected it. Congress reintroduced the proposal the next year, coupling it with a number of others to make it more agreeable to the states' wishes. By 1786, all of the states, except New York, had voted in favor of

the amendment, but again the need for unanimous decision killed the proposal. Another weakness of the Articles had been made evident—the need for all states to agree on amendments. The Constitution would make amendment easier.

The inadequacy of Congress contributed to a sharp decline in its prestige. Fewer and fewer representatives attended meetings. At some meetings, no business could take place because Congress lacked the required number of members to hold session.

If Congress was weak, the executive and judiciary were nonexistent. Because there was no executive branch, Congress's time was taken up by administrative duties. The lack of a judiciary system meant that the national government had to rely on state courts to enforce national laws. In practice, this gave state courts the power to overturn national laws. George Washington was among those who saw state sovereignty as a threat: "I do not conceive we can exist long as a nation without having lodged somewhere a power which will pervade the whole Union in as energetic a manner as the authority of the state governments extends over the several states."[50]

THE FOREIGN THREAT

The fledgling confederation was also threatened by foreign powers. The European countries refused to lower their barriers to free trade, which would help ease America's commercial problems. Without a navy, the newly independent states were unable to stop pirates from raiding American vessels on the high seas. Spain, which owned the land west of the Mississippi, refused to allow Americans navigational rights on the Mississippi River. "From this new and wonderful system of government," wrote John Jay, "it has come to pass, that . . . other nations taking advantage of its imbecility, are daily multiplying commercial restraints upon us."[51]

England refused to comply with provisions of the Treaty of Paris that required the removal of British soldiers from forts in the American colonies and stationed additional troops along the northern border to coerce the United States to repay its debts according to the treaty provisions. Another war with Britain threatened.

Thomas Jefferson, who was serving as ambassador to France, and John Adams, ambassador to England, reported that the confederation inspired little respect in Europe. European diplomats pointedly asked about Congress's power to appoint ambassadors and questioned whether a state would be able to undermine or negate treaties made with the confederate United States. In a letter home, Jefferson lamented that he and his fellow commissioners were "the lowest and most obscure of the whole diplomatic tribe. . . . We do not find it easy to make commercial arrangements in Europe. There is a wont of confidence in us."[52] According to Jefferson, the confederation needed "to take the commerce of the states out of the hands of the states, and to place it under the superintendence of Congress."[53]

ECONOMIC WOES SPUR REBELLION

A severe depression in 1785–1786 increased economic hardship among the states and spurred price increases. Most people in the new states were farmers, and many of them had serious debts. Under the laws in effect at that time, debtors were imprisoned and their land was confiscated. In western Massachusetts, where many farmers were angry also over the eastern dominance of the legislature, Daniel Shays, a farmer who had served as captain during the American Revolution, led upward of twelve hundred men in an armed rebellion.

Shays's Rebellion was quelled in a matter of days, but it caused alarm throughout the states and pointed out inadequacies in the existing government. The uprising un-

Shays's Rebellion highlighted America's need for a stronger national government.

Shays's Rebellion Spurs Nationalism

Shays's Rebellion served as a catalyst for those who wanted a strong central government. The following letter from John Jay to Thomas Jefferson, written in October 1786, echoed the feelings of those who feared what would happen if a stronger government was not put into place. This excerpt is taken from Winthrop D. Jordan's and Leon F. Littwack's The United States.

"The inefficacy of our Government becomes daily more and more apparent. Our Credit and our Treasury are in a sad Situation, and it is probable that either the Wisdom or the Passions of the People will produce Changes.

A Spirit of Licentiousness has infected Massachusetts, which appears more formidable than some at first apprehended; whether similar Symptoms will soon mark a like Disease in several other States, is very problematical.

[W]e are in a very unpleasant Situation. Changes are Necessary, but what they ought to be, what they will be, and how and when to be produced, are arduous Questions. I feel for the Cause of Liberty and for the Honor of my Countrymen who have so nobly asserted it, and who at present so abuse its Blessings. If it should not take Root in this Soil little Pains will be taken to cultivate it in any other."

derscored the growing understanding that a stronger central government was imperative to maintain order and to direct the economy. In a letter to James Madison, George Washington wrote of his opinion that the uprising signaled a need for a new government:

Without some alteration in our political creed, the superstructure we have been seven years raising at the expence of much blood and treasure, must fall. We are fast verging to anarchy and confusion! . . . How melancholy is the reflection that in so short a space, we should have made such large strides towards fulfilling the prediction of our transatlantic foes!— "leave them to themselves, and their government will soon dissolve." . . . Thirteen Sovereignties pulling against each other, and all tugging at the federal head, will soon bring ruin on the whole; whereas a liberal, and energetic Constitution, well guarded and closely watched to prevent encroachments, might restore us to that degree of respectability and consequence to which we had a fair claim and the brightest prospect of attaining.[54]

The nation could not long exist, wrote Washington, "without having lodged some where a power, which will pervade

A Crisis of Authority

Reacting to Shays's Rebellion, the American Recorder, *a Charleston, Massachusetts, newspaper, published an editorial on March 16, 1787, arguing that events demonstrated the need for a stronger national government. This excerpt is taken from William Dudley's* The Creation of the Constitution.

"This is a crisis in our affairs, which requires all the wisdom and energy of government; for every man of sense must be convinced that our disturbances have arisen, more from a want of power, than the abuse of it—from the relaxation, and almost annihilation of our federal government—from the feeble, unsystematic, temporising, inconstant character of our own state—from the derangement of our finances—the oppressive absurdity of our mode of taxation—and from the astonishing enthusiasm and perversion of principles among the people. It is not extraordinary that commotions have been excited. It is strange, that under the circumstances which we have been discussing, that they did not appear sooner, and terminate more fatally. For let it be remarked, that a feeble government produces more factions than an oppressive one. The want of power first makes individuals pretended legislators, and then, active rebels. Where parents want authority, children are wanting in duty. It is not possible to advance further in the same path. Here the ways divide, the one will conduct us to anarchy, and next to foreign or domestic tyranny: the other, by the wise and vigorous exertion of lawful authority, will lead to permanent power, and general prosperity. I am no advocate for despotism; but I believe the probability to be much less of its being introduced by the corruption of our rules, than by the delusion of the people. . . .

While the bands of union are so loose, we are no more entitled to the character of a nation than the hordes of vagabond traitors. Reason has ever condemned our paltry prejudices upon this important subject. Now that experience has come in aid of reason, let us renounce them. For what is there now to prevent our subjugation by a foreign power, but their contempt of the acquisition? It is time to render the federal head supreme in the United States."

the whole Union in as energetic a manner as the authority of the State Government extends over the several states."[55]

Not everyone reacted as strongly as George Washington. When Abigail Adams sent word of Shays's Rebellion to Thomas Jefferson, he replied,

> The spirit of resistance to government is so valuable on certain occasions, that I wish it to be always kept alive. It will often be exercised when wrong, but better so than not to be exercised at all. I like a little rebellion now and then. It is like a storm in the atmosphere.[56]

MOVING BEYOND THE ARTICLES

Disputes among the states continued to hamper trade. In August 1786, James Madison, a young congressman from Virginia, called for a meeting to settle trade issues—particularly the ongoing dispute between Virginia and Maryland regarding the navigation of the Potomac River. At his urging, a meeting was held in Annapolis, Maryland.

Alexander Hamilton had long been an advocate of a strong central government. Like Washington, he believed that it was impossible to govern through thirteen sovereign states. For many years, Hamilton had been campaigning for a constitutional convention. As early as 1780, he had sent a seventeen-page letter to a member of the Continental Congress calling the system under the Articles "neither fit for war nor peace" and blaming "an excess of the spirit of liberty which had made the particular states show a jealousy of all power not in their hands."[57] He expanded upon his letter to express his opinions in a six-part newspaper series penned by the "Continentalist," in which he outlined the defects of the Articles and called for a convention. Hamilton saw his opening at the meeting in Annapolis. At his urging, the delegates asked Congress to hold a meeting to revise the Articles.

Congress sanctioned the convention with a resolution and invited states to send delegates "to take into consideration the situation of the United States, to devise such further provisions as shall appear to them necessary to render the constitution of the Federal Government adequate to the exigencies of the Union."[58] The "Grand Convention" or "Federal Convention," as it was referred to, would be held in Philadelphia in May 1787. Although at the time people believed the purpose of that meeting was to revise the Articles of Confederation, in fact, a new constitution was born. Thus, the historic meeting in Philadelphia has become better known as the "Constitutional Convention."

4 The Road to Philadelphia

At the request of the delegations at Annapolis, Congress passed a resolution for revising the Articles of Confederation and issued an invitation to the thirteen new states to send delegates to a meeting in Philadelphia. Twelve of the thirteen states heeded the call. Despite opposition to the convention among many, only Rhode Island refused to send delegates.

The states were invited to send as many people as they wanted. Of the seventy-one people nominated by the state legislatures, fifty-five attended the convention. Pennsylvania's delegation of eight was the largest; Virginia sent seven delegates; the tiny state of Delaware sent five.

The task that confronted the delegates was not an easy one. A month before the convention, James Madison wrote, "The necessity of gaining the concurrence of the Convention in some system that will answer the purpose, the subsequent approbation of Congress, and the final sanction of the states, presents a series of chances which would inspire despair in any case where the alternative was less formidable."[59] Madison agreed with other Federalists that the failure to form a stronger national government would be the new nation's demise.

OPPOSITION TO THE CONVENTION

Not all of the new nation's great patriots attended the Constitutional Convention. Thomas Jefferson and John Adams were unable to attend because they were serving as ambassadors in Europe. Both maintained an active interest in the proceedings, however, and sent letters, books, and advice.

Others refused to attend because of their opposition to strengthening the role of the national government. As historian Fred Barbash explains, "In 1787, only a handful of enthusiasts were committed to a new government. The spirit of '76 was far different than '87."[60] Patrick Henry was among those who declined to attend, saying he "smelled a rat." A staunch supporter of the American Revolution, Henry believed that the convention would deprive the states of their legitimate authority. Later, during the ratification process, Henry became a vocal advocate for adding a bill of rights.

Samuel Adams, a Boston merchant who had led Massachusetts in defiance of British rule, also declined an invitation to attend. During the process of ratification in Massachusetts, Adams opposed the new constitution vigorously. "I stumble at the threshold," he wrote. "I meet with a national government instead of a federal union of sovereign states."[61]

Congress, still sitting in New York, was often suspicious of the proceedings in Philadelphia. Some representatives expressed their dismay of losing members to the convention, particularly when they realized that it would drag on through the summer. William Grayson, a congressman from Virginia, wrote "I hardly think much good can come of it. The people of America don't appear to me to be ripe for any great innovations."[62]

What would have happened if these and other vocal opponents of a strong central government had attended the meeting in Philadelphia? Historians can only speculate, but given the nature of the debate, the convention might well have adjourned without resolution.

Samuel Adams declined to attend the Constitutional Convention because he opposed a strong national government.

"AN ASSEMBLY OF DEMIGODS"

George Washington at first declined Virginia's nomination to attend the convention. After the war, Washington had announced his retirement to tend to Mount Vernon, his seven-thousand-acre farm. In response to Virginia's invitation, Washington wrote: "Retired as I am from the world, I frankly acknowledge that I cannot feel myself an unconcerned spectator. Yet having happily assisted in bringing the Ship into Port . . . it is not my business to embark again on the sea of troubles."[63]

James Madison and other colleagues begged him to reconsider. Washington's success as a general during the Revolutionary War had brought him fame and enormous respect, and advocates of the meeting believed that his acceptance would send a message to others that this was an important event. James Madison observed that failing to secure Washington as a Virginia delegate would "probably frustrate the whole scheme."[64] In the end, Washington relented. Not only did he attend the convention, he provided an invaluable service as president over the proceedings.

Present at the Constitutional Convention were a number of other men who had made clear their arguments for a strong central government. Alexander Hamilton, who had argued that a constitutional convention was needed for many years prior to the convention, represented New York. Benjamin Franklin, who had called for union in Albany more than thirty years before, attended as part of Pennsylvania's delegation. And, of course, there was

A Pessimistic Outlook

Not everyone agreed that the Philadelphia convention would be successful. In a letter to James Monroe, William Grayson, a congressman from Virginia, describes his belief that nothing will come from the meeting because a strong government was not in the states' economic interests. This excerpt is reprinted from Jane Nevins's Turning 200: A Bicentennial History of the Rise of the American Republic.

"What will be the result of [the Philadelphia] meeting, I cannot with any certainty determine, but I hardly think much good can come of it. The people of America don't appear to me to be ripe for any great innovations, and it seems they are ultimately to ratify or reject.

In Massachusetts, they think that government is too strong and are about rebelling again, for the purpose of making it more democratical. In Connecticut, they have rejected [paying to support Congress] decidedly, and no man there would be elected to the office of constable if he was to declare that he meant to pay a copper towards the domestic debt. Rhode Island has refused to send members. . . .

New Hampshire has not paid a shilling since peace and does not ever mean to pay one to all eternity—if it was attempted to tax the people for the domestic debt, 500 Shays would arise in a fortnight. In New York they pay well because they can do it by plundering New Jersey and Connecticut. Jersey will go great lengths from motives of revenge and Interest. Pennsylvania will join provided you let the sessions of the Executive of America be fixed in Philadelphia and give her other advantages in trade to compensate for the loss of State power. I shall make no observations on the southern States, but I think they will be (perhaps from different motives) as little disposed to part with efficient power as any in the Union."

James Madison, a young lawyer and politician from Virginia, whose steady work in favor of union earned him the moniker "father of the Constitution."

The delegates were an illustrious group. George Mason, a delegate from Virginia, wrote, "America has certainly, upon this occasion, drawn forth her first characters."[65] When he received the list of attendees,

Thomas Jefferson wrote to John Adams that it was "an assembly of demigods."

Common Bonds

The delegates came from a variety of backgrounds. They were lawyers, merchants, farmers, plantation owners, physicians, politicians, financiers, and political scientists—and more often than not, several of the above.

As a whole, the group was well-educated. Perhaps more importantly, they were experienced. Almost all had served in a colonial or state legislature, and most had spent some time in service at the Continental Congress. Eight had signed the Declaration of Independence. At least thirty had served in the Revolutionary War. Several had experience developing the constitutions of their states, bills of rights, the Articles of Confederation, and other documents of freedom. John Dickinson, a delegate from Delaware, for example, had formulated the Declaration of Rights and Grievances at the Stamp Act Congress in 1765 and the first draft of the Articles of Confederation. "Experience must be our only guide," he advised. "Reason may mislead us."[66] As historians Oscar and Lilian Handlin explain, "For the task at hand, intellectual brilliance counted for less than the knack for practical compromise."[67]

This common experience gave the delegates a unique worldly perspective. They had learned about the opinions and lifestyles of those living in other states or regions and were more likely to consider themselves citizens of America than of their independent states. In working together to defeat England, they had learned to listen, to discuss, and to compromise, and they had witnessed the advantage of working together toward common goals. "Over the years," writes one historian, "the men devoted to the Congress had become a kind of brotherhood."[68]

THE PHILOSOPHICAL FOUNDATION

The ideas and opinions of the men who met in Philadelphia in 1787 were influenced by the Enlightenment, a movement that focused on the strength of reason and respect for human dignity. The Enlightenment, which swept through Europe and the colonies during the decades prior to the American Revolution, built on the ideas of earlier political philosophers, including Thomas Hobbes and John Locke. The general ideas of the Enlightenment were part of a common base of understanding from which the delegates worked. They looked to the works of John Locke, Charles de Montesquieu, Jean-Jacques Rousseau, and others for guidance about how to make governments responsive to the will of the people and how to restrain governments from interfering with civil rights and liberties.

Political philosopher John Locke captured the essence of the Enlightenment in his writings, which heavily influenced the men who drafted the Constitution.

Delegates at the Constitutional Convention

Fifty-five delegates representing twelve of the thirteen existing states converged in Philadelphia during the hot summer of 1787. Each brought his own unique knowledge, experiences, and ideas. Although the average delegate was only thirty-three, each had already gathered a wealth of experience. Most of the delegates had experience in politics or government and made a living as merchants, lawyers, farmers, and the like. The states are listed in the order in which their delegates signed the document. The asterisks indicate delegates who were not present when the document was signed or who chose not to sign it.

New Hampshire: John Langdon, Nicholas Gilman

Massachusetts: Elbridge Gerry*, Nathaniel Gorham, Rufus King, Caleb Strong*

Connecticut: William Samuel Johnson, Roger Sherman, Oliver Ellsworth*

New York: Robert Yates*, John Lansing Jr.*, Alexander Hamilton

New Jersey: William Livingston, David Brearley, William Churchill Houston*, William Paterson, Jonathon Dayton

Pennsylvania: Thomas Mifflin, Robert Morris, George Clymer, Jared Ingersoll, Thomas Fitzsimons, James Wilson, Gouverneur Morris, Benjamin Franklin, Francis Hopkinson

Delaware: George Read, John Dickinson, Gunning Bedford Jr., Richard Bassett, Jacob Broom

Maryland: James McHenry, Daniel of St. Thomas Jenifer, Daniel Carroll, John Francis Mercer*, Luther Martin*

Virginia: George Washington, Edmund Randolph*, John Blair*, James Madison, George Mason*, George Wythe*, James McClurg*

North Carolina: William Blount, Alexander Martin*, William Richardson Davie, Richard Dobbs Spaight, Hugh Williamson

South Carolina: John Rutledge, Charles Cotesworth Pinckney, Pierce Butler

Georgia: William Few, Abraham Baldwin, William Pierce*, William Houstoun

The ideas of John Locke, an English philosopher, were particularly influential during the eighteenth century. In his *Two Treatises of Government*, written in 1690, Locke argued that sovereignty did not reside in the state, but rather with the people, and denounced the concept that kings were granted their power by divine right. He explained that people voluntarily give up some freedom in order to have clear laws and impartial judges. The government has the right to govern only as long as it adheres to a person's "natural" rights. Locke supported revolution, claiming that it was not only a right but often an obligation, and he defended religious freedom and the separation of church and state. Many of his political ideas, including those relating to natural rights, property rights, the duty of the government to protect these rights, and the rule of the majority, were incorporated into the U.S. Constitution.

Charles de Montesquieu, a French writer and jurist, spent several years studying the British system of government. In his 1748 work, *The Spirit of Laws*, Montesquieu held that governmental powers should be separated and balanced to guarantee individual rights and freedom. He believed that power within the British system was well distributed among the king, the House of Commons, and the House of Lords. Montesquieu argued that abuse of power, slavery, and intolerance were evil. He believed that government can avoid these evils by separating power into executive, legislative, and judicial branches, by governing with honor rather than through fear, and by upholding human dignity. James Madison indicated that Montesquieu was a main inspiration for the theory of separation of powers included in the U.S. Constitution.

Jean-Jacques Rousseau, an eighteenth-century French musician, writer, philosopher, and political theorist, contributed greatly to the movement in Western Europe for individual freedom. In his 1762 book, *The Social Contract*, he maintained that no laws are binding unless agreed upon by the people. His staunch defense of civil liberties and the popular will against divine right is often considered one of the chief forces that brought on the French Revolution in the late eighteenth century.

AGREEMENT AND DISAGREEMENT

For the most part, the delegates agreed about their mission. They recognized the need for a written document that would bind the states together and serve as the law of the land. They looked for the best way to accomplish this without overriding the rights of citizens. In the process, they embarked on a journey to forge a new system of government—outlining a new system of government uniquely crafted to meet the needs and concerns of their fellow countrymen.

As historian James MacGregor Burns explains,

> The delegates did not see themselves as merely landowners or merchants or lawyers. They conceived of themselves as engaged in a grand "experiment"—a word they often used—the outcome of which would shape their nation's destiny, and hence their own and their posterity's, for decades to come. They saw themselves—in a word they would never have used—as pragmatists, as men thinking their way through a thicket of problems in pursuit of that goal. That goal was liberty—liberty with order, liberty with safety and security, liberty of

conscience, liberty of property, liberty with a measure of equality, but above all, liberty. . . . [L]iberty served as a unifying symbol and goal around which practical men could rally.[69]

The delegates agreed also that liberty as described in the Declaration of Independence could be secured only through a republican government that derived its power from the consent of the governed. Their experience under colonial rule and under the Articles of Confederation had shown them that their greatest challenge was to set up a government with enough power to act while protecting the rights of citizens against tyranny. "In framing a government which is to be administered by men over men," wrote James Madison, "the great difficulty lies in this: you must first enable the government to control the governed; and in the next place oblige it to control itself."[70]

Most of the delegates came to the convention with their own opinions—opinions that were forged from solid experience. Delegates who had served in the Continental Congress and had witnessed the inadequacy of government under the Articles of Confederation typically wanted to see that any changes to the system of government strengthened the role of that national body.

However, not everyone favored a strong national government. Robert Yates and John Lansing Jr., who represented New York, were opposed to making the national government stronger and left in protest when it became clear that this was the way the convention was headed. Sev-

eral of the smaller states were concerned that they would be swallowed up by the larger states. The state of Delaware forbade its delegates to change Article V, which guaranteed each state one vote. Again and again throughout the four months of the convention, the delegates discussed their differences. Again and again, they succeeded in forging compromise.

PREPARING FOR THE CONVENTION

By the time they met in Philadelphia, the delegates had thought long and hard about what they wanted to accomplish. It was by no means clear how to go about creating a government that would be adequate for the growing country, particularly since the new Americans clearly opposed a monarchy. Historians Oscar and Lilian Handlin interpret the dilemma which the delegates confronted:

The precedents of ancient confederacies and modern European leagues offered meager encouragement, since history and political theory taught Americans that while small states like the Greek or Roman cities or Venice or the cantons of Switzerland could function as republics, only a monarchy could maintain order in a vast territory. . . . Republics like Sparta, pure and strong while young and small, lost virtue and power with the increase in size and luxury.[71]

During the ratification debate Virginia delegate George Mason summed up the quandary:

It is ascertained, by history, that there never was a government over a very extensive country without destroying the liberties of the people: history also, supported by the opinions of the best writers, shows us that monarchy may suit a large territory, and despotic governments over so extensive a country, but that popular governments can only exist in small territories. Is there a single example, on the face of the earth, to support a contrary opinion? . . . Was there ever an instance of a general national government extending over so extensive a country, abounding in such a variety of climates, etc., where the people retained their liberty?[72]

As the convention neared, the delegates thought about how to solve these problems—how exactly to create a republic that would be able to govern such a large and growing nation. The North Carolina delegation reported from the convention that "A very large field presents to our view without a single straight or eligible road that has been trodden by the feet of nations."[73]

No one prepared more diligently than Virginia's James Madison. At Madison's request, Jefferson had sent hundreds of books—books on government and political theory, encyclopedias, histories, biographies, and memoirs. Throughout the winter, Madison read from this vast library, taking meticulous notes. He analyzed the governments of ancient civilizations and modern nations—including the American confederacy. In a

George Mason, delegate to the Constitutional Convention, outlined the difficulties of maintaining order in a large country while still providing for personal liberties.

letter to Washington that he wrote well over a month before the convention, Madison outlined the most important points to be discussed and decided. He also laid out the system to be used to agree on a new constitution—the system of ratification that was used put the document into effect.

CONVERGING ON PHILADELPHIA

The delegates set out for Philadelphia in the spring of 1787, some with their wives and children. The journey was often long and arduous, and rain and muddy roads hampered their progress. Some of the delegates traveled for weeks on horseback, by stagecoach, or along the coast in schooners.

For the Record

"I chose a seat in front of the presiding member, with the other members on my right and left hand. In this favorable position for hearing all that passed, I noted in terms legible and in abbreviations and marks intelligible to myself what was read from the Chair or spoken by the members; and losing not a moment unnecessarily between the adjournment and reassembling of the Convention I was enabled to write out my daily notes during the session or within a few finishing days after its close in the extent and form preserved in my own hand on my files. . . . I was not absent a single day, nor more than a casual fraction of an hour in any day, so that I could not have lost a single speech, unless a very short one."

Throughout the Constitutional Convention, James Madison took meticulous notes of the proceedings.

Throughout May and June, the delegates trickled into Philadelphia. The New Hampshire delegation did not arrive until eight weeks after the convention began because the state was too poor to pay their expenses. The last delegate, John Francis Mercer, did not arrive until August 6.

On May 14, the day the convention was expected to open, only Pennsylvania and Virginia had delegations in Philadelphia. James Madison, the first delegate to reach Philadelphia, had arrived three weeks early, armed with notes and papers from his winter of study, and the other members of his delegation soon joined him. As they waited for the other delegations to arrive, the Virginians held daily meetings "in order to form a proper correspondence of sentiments; and to grow into some acquaintance with each other."[74] At these meetings, the Virginia delegates drafted the resolves that became known as the Virginia Plan.

"Pray Hurry On"

Over the next few weeks, the delegates streamed into Philadelphia, where they joined others for casual discussions about the agenda for the convention. The early arrivals begged the other members of their delegations to join them. Delaware delegate George Read wrote to a straggler in his delegation:

> I wish you were here. I suspect it to be of importance to the small states that their deputies should keep a strict watch upon the movements and propositions from the larger States, who will probably combine to swallow up the smaller ones . . . and, if you have any wish to assist in guarding against such attempts, you will be speedy in your attendance.[75]

Rufus King of Massachusetts found himself outnumbered also. "I am mortified that I alone am from New England," he wrote to his fellow delegates. "The Backwardness may prove unfortunate. Pray hurry on your Delegates."[76]

THE MIGHTY PEN

The ideas that circulated among the early delegates did not confine themselves to a modest revision of government. Some recommended dividing the United States into four districts. Others began to talk about an executive branch. Some of the delegates expected little from the convention, but the sentiment that they were about to embark on a second revolution began to take hold in others. George Mason expressed this opinion:

> The eyes of the United States are turned upon this assembly and their expectations raised to a very anxious degree.

May God grant we may be able to gratify them by establishing a wise and just government. . . . The revolt from Great Britain and the formations of our new governments at that time, were nothing compared to the great business now before us. There was then a certain degree of enthusiasm, which inspired and supported the mind. But to view, through the calm, sedate medium of reason, the influence which the establishment now proposed may have upon the happiness or misery of millions yet unborn, is an object of such magnitude as . . . suspends the operations of human understanding.[77]

If the weapon of the first revolution had been the musket, the weapon of the constitutional revolution was to be the mighty pen.

Delegate George Read of Delaware feared that the larger states at the convention would jeopardize the interests of smaller states.

5 The Constitutional Convention

Despite its subsequent indisputable success as a governing document, the provisions of the Constitution were vehemently debated both at the convention in Philadelphia and at the state conventions called to ratify the document. Debates pitted large states against small, North against South, advocates of a strong central government against states' rights advocates.

The Constitutional Convention turned out to be a long meeting. The delegates worked laboriously in the hot Pennsylvania statehouse to "create a more perfect union." At times, it looked as though divisive issues would prove to be too much and the threat of dissolution without solution would loom. As mentioned earlier, many delegates were late arriving, and some left periodically for home to attend to business or deal with family illnesses. By July 8, all three of New York's delegates had decamped, and only Alexander Hamilton would return. Robert Yates and John Lansing stayed away to protest the direction the convention was headed. Through its choices of delegates, New York had nullified much of Hamilton's influence. As George Mason wrote after the convention, "Yates and Lansing never voted *in one single instance* with Hamilton,

who was so much mortified at it that he went home."[78] Luther Martin, a Maryland delegate, also left in a huff, although much later in the summer. "I'll be hanged if the people of Maryland ever agree to [the Constitution],"[79] he announced.

But most of the delegates were committed to the cause. Only through the unflagging determination of this handful of men did the U.S. Constitution become a reality. On a series of critical issues—representation, state equality and authority, the mode of electing the president and representatives, the method of counting slaves for representation, and other issues—the men in Philadelphia worked together for seventeen long, hot weeks to reach compromise solutions. As a result, the U.S. Constitution has sometimes been called a "bundle of compromises."

THE CONVENTION BEGINS

By May 25, a quorum of seven states had finally arrived. The convention opened in the Pennsylvania State House—the building known today as Independence Hall.

On the first day of the convention, George Washington was unanimously elected to preside over the convention. Washington proved to be as adept at leading in the convention as he had been on the battlefield. As presiding officer, he was silent during most of the meeting, but delegates said they could read his opinion through his countenance. Also, he had made clear his desire for a strong national government well before the convention began.

After the delegations introduced themselves, they began to lay the ground rules for the conduct of the meeting. The rules were simple. A quorum of seven states would be required to transact business. Each state had one vote, regardless of its population, size or number of delegates, and could cast its vote only if a majority of its delegates were present. Decisions would be made by simple majority of the states present. The delegates also enacted a rule that provided for reconsideration of matters that had already been passed by the majority. This allowed the delegates to again discuss issues that were affected by later decisions and to change their minds. Throughout the convention, this rule often came into effect as the delegates debated, discussed, voted, and reconsidered, issues. Allowing reconsideration of issues gave delegates the opportunity to change their minds when new information warranted.

The delegates also agreed to keep their deliberations secret. The secrecy rule allowed delegates to speak more freely and insulated them from outside influences. Thomas Jefferson, looking on from France, said he hated the secrecy rule because government by the people should always be conducted openly. James Madison countered that the delegates were not engaged in government but in building a government. Several years later Madison wrote of the rule:

> Much was to be gained by a yielding and accommodating spirit. Had the members committed themselves publicly at first, they would have

The Consitutional Convention met at the Philadelphia State House, today known as Independence Hall.

VIRGINIA SETS THE STAGE

At the opening of the Philadelphia convention, each delegation introduced itself and gave its credentials. Some of the delegations read the resolutions that had been prepared by their state legislatures, reiterating the purpose of the meeting. In this excerpt reprinted in Catherine Drinker Bowen's Miracle at Philadelphia, *the Virginia delegation gives its opinion of the enormous significance of the meeting.*

"The Crisis is arrived at which the good People of America are to decide the solemn question whether they will by just and magnanimous Efforts reap the just fruits of that Independence which they have so gloriously acquired and of that Union which they have cemented with so much of their common Blood, or whether by giving way to unmanly Jealousies and Prejudices or to partial and transitory Interests they will . . . furnish our Enemies with cause to triumph."

afterwards supposed consistency required them to maintain their ground. Whereas, by secret discussion, no man felt himself obligated to retain his opinions any longer than he was satisfied of their propriety and truth, and was open to the force of argument.[80]

EARLY PROPOSALS

On May 29, the convention was ready to begin what they had come to do—fix the Articles of Confederation. Governor Edmund Randolph of Virginia addressed the convention. Using notes from his meetings with the Virginia delegation, Randolph analyzed the list of defects in the Articles, which he declared had been devised during "the infancy of the science of constitutions."[81] Then he proposed fifteen resolutions to correct these problems, based on what the Virginians had discussed prior to the convention. The plan was not designed to be an end product, but a starting point for discussion. Madison later called the Virginia Plan "a mere sketch in which omitted details were to be supplied, and the general terms and phrases to be reduced to their proper details."[82] The delegates would spend the rest of the summer analyzing, debating, and revising each resolve.

The so-called Virginia Plan was a radical departure from the Articles of Confederation. Congress would have two houses, with the number of representatives decided according to state population. Under the Virginia Plan, members of both houses would vote as individuals rather than as members of a state voting bloc. The Virginia Plan added an executive branch and a judicial branch—both of which would be selected by Congress.

Charles Pinckney, a wealthy planter representing South Carolina, also presented on the first day of the convention a plan for resolving the Union's problems. As it was late in the day, the convention broke up before either of the plans was discussed. As it turned out, Pinckney's plan was never discussed.

THE MEETING BECOMES A CONSTITUTIONAL CONVENTION

When the convention reconvened the next day, it met as a Committee of the Whole to discuss the Virginia Plan. The Committee of the Whole—a "committee" of all the delegates—was a device first used by the British Parliament and adopted by the Continental Congress. It allowed members to discuss issues frankly and to take informal votes to get an overview of delegate attitudes. The Committee of the Whole could

then propose resolutions to the convention for a "real" vote. This system enabled the delegates to work out difficult issues.

When the convention met as a Committee of the Whole, George Washington always stepped down from his chair as president and joined the Virginia delegation. Nathaniel Gorham of Massachusetts assumed Washington's place for the debates.

Often during the convention, work was accomplished "out of doors," a phrase the delegates used for any discussions that took place beyond the walls of Independence Hall. That very first evening an important change had come about as a result of out-of-doors discussions. Reviewing the day's work, Gouverneur Morris, a delegate from Pennsylvania, argued that the resolves Randolph had recommended in fact called for a new system of government, not a revision of the Articles. He felt that the first resolve, which read that "the articles of Confederation ought to be so corrected and

The delegates to the Constitutional Convention meeting as a Committee of the Whole.

Charles Pinckney worried that the convention might lead to the complete abolition of state governments.

enlarged to accomplish the objects proposed by their institution; namely, common defence, security of liberty and general welfare,"[83] should use stronger language to reflect the change that Randolph proposed.

The next day, May 30, Randolph took up Morris's suggestion. Randolph turned attention again to the first resolve of the Virginia Plan, which declared to the convention that "a union of the states . . . will not accomplish the objects proposed by the articles,"[84] and proposed instead "a national government, consisting of a supreme legislative, executive and judicial."[85]

A hush fell over the room. The thought that they were about to begin by throwing out the Articles rather than simply revising them surprised the delegates. Charles Pinckney of South Carolina rose to ask whether Randolph "meant to abolish the State Governments altogether."[86] Others worried that this was going beyond the authority given to them by the state legislatures "for the sole and express purpose" of revising the Articles. "It is questionable," posited Elbridge Gerry of Massachusetts, ". . . whether this convention can propose a government totally different or whether Congress itself would have a right to pass such a resolution. . . . If we have a right to pass this resolution, we have a right to annihilate the confederation."[87]

George Washington told the delegates to trust their own opinions about what they expected to accomplish and the best way to reach their goals. The matter boiled down to whether they should write a new constitution that would meet the needs of the people or, instead, proceed to revise the Articles even if the revision would do little to improve the current situation. In the end, the delegates agreed to Governor Randolph's proposal to write a new constitution. With the passage of this resolution, the gathering at Independence Hall became a constitutional convention.

THE VIRGINIA PLAN

Once the delegates had agreed that they were developing a new constitution, they turned their attention to other aspects of the Virginia Plan. They agreed with the proposal that the national government have three separate divisions—executive, legislative, and judicial. This was familiar, as it was the system in many of the state governments. They also agreed to have a bicameral, or two-house, legislature, the system in place in all the states except Pennsylvania.

However, many of the resolutions were more problematic. The Virginia Plan recommended that representation to the legislature be based on population—a proposal some states vehemently opposed and one that would take half the summer to resolve. A dark cloud also threatened when the delegates turned their attention to slavery—an increasingly alienating issue between the northern and southern states. These issues proved to be difficult and divisive. At several times during the days to come, the convention found itself at a standstill and it appeared that the delegates would go home without success. At these times, the delegates would remind one another of the dangers that the young country faced—the external and internal pressures threatening to break it apart—and rehash the issues again and again until compromise could be forged.

THE NEW JERSEY PLAN

The delegates spent the next two weeks considering each clause of the Virginia Plan. On the morning of June 14, the day

---

AN INSIDER'S VIEW

A month after the convention began, the delegates discussed and debated the Virginia Plan. It was clear to many that a new form of government was being forged—and that the work of the convention was not near an end. As the convention took a break to allow New Jersey and other states to come up with an alternative plan to the Virginia Plan, the delegation from North Carolina wrote to their governor. As recounted by Catherine Drinker Bowen in Miracle at Philadelphia, *they give their opinion of how things are going.*

"Though we sit from day to day, Saturdays included, it is not possible for us to determine when the business before us can be finished, a very large field presents to our view without a single straight or eligible road that has been trodden by the feet of nations. An union of sovereign states, preserving their civil liberties and connected together by such ties as to preserve permanent and effective governments is a system not described, it is a circumstance that has not occurred in the history of men.

Several members of the convention have their wives here and other gentlemen have sent for theirs. This seems to promise a summer's campaign. Such of us as can remain here from the inevitable avocation of private business, are resolved to continue whilst there is any prospect of being able to serve the state and union."

that a vote on the Virginia Plan was to be taken, William Paterson of New Jersey announced that several of the delegations wanted to propose an alternative plan. He was granted a day's recess to prepare it.

Paterson's plan, which became known as the New Jersey Plan, reversed the direction the convention was headed. It called for a return to a more moderate revision of the Articles of Confederation. The New Jersey Plan would address the weaknesses of the Articles by giving the Confederation Congress authority to impose taxes and to regulate commerce among the states and with foreign countries. The plan proposed an executive branch headed by more than one person and a supreme court with limited juris-

William Paterson of New Jersey suggested that a more moderate approach for the convention was needed and proposed that the delegates merely revise the Articles of Confederation.

diction. Under the plan, there would continue to be a single legislative body that would get its power from the states and not the people. The state legislatures would continue to appoint and pay delegates, for example. Most importantly, each state would continue to have one vote in Congress.

Opponents of the New Jersey Plan argued that it did not go far enough to rectify problems with the Articles of Confederation. The plan did not address how conflicts among states would be resolved. It offered states no assistance in dealing with civil unrest or outbreaks like Shays's Rebellion. It did little to strengthen ties among the states or provide for a common defense or a stable economy. Delegate George Read said that modifying the old system "would be like putting new cloth on an old garment."[88]

On the afternoon of June 19, the Committee of the Whole voted to submit a revised version of the Virginia Plan. The delegates had decided that it was too hard to patch up the Articles of Confederation. They also realized that it would take additional time to resolve the many issues that had come to light during the discussions of the past several weeks. In fact, even though they had the skeleton of the Virginia Plan from which to build, it would take them another three months to finalize a plan to propose to Congress.

A NATIONAL GOVERNMENT

States' rights advocates hated the Virginia Plan. They worried that it would be the end to the state governments and argued

ONE NATION OF BRETHREN

James Wilson was among the delegates who argued for a strong national government. In the following speech made at the Constitutional Convention, he calls on delegates to remember the forces that united them during the American Revolution. This excerpt is taken from Catherine Drinker Bowen's Miracle at Philadelphia.

"We must remember the language with which we began the Revolution: 'Virginia is no more, Massachusetts is no more, Pennsylvania is no more. We are now one nation of brethren, we must bury all local interests and distinctions. . . .'

[But] the tables at length began to turn. No sooner were the state governments formed than their jealousy and ambition began to display themselves. Each endeavored to cut a slice from the common loaf to add to its own morsel, 'til at length the Confederation became frittered down to the important condition in which it now stands. Review the progress of the Articles of Confederation through Congress. . . . One of its vices is the want of an effectual control in the whole over its parts. What danger is there that the whole will unnecessarily sacrifice a part? But reverse the case, and leave the whole at the mercy of each part, and will not the general interest be continually sacrificed to local interests?"

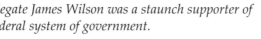

Delegate James Wilson was a staunch supporter of a federal system of government.

that the people would have little say in a far-removed national government.

Other delegates pointed out that the bickering and jealousies among the states were the source of many of the problems of the Union. "I do not see the danger of the states being devoured by the national government," wrote James Wilson, a respected judge and scholar. "On the contrary, I wish to keep them [the states] from devouring the national government."[89]

The convention proposed a system by which the state and national governments could coexist. The people would be citizens of both their national and their state governments. "I am both a citizen of Pennsylvania and of the United States,"[90] explained Wilson. This, in short, was the principle of federalism.

Under the system proposed, only some powers would be turned over to the national government, while the states would retain sovereignty in others. "Let our government be like that of the solar system," suggested John Dickinson, a delegate from Delaware, who had drafted the Articles of Confederation. "Let the general government be like the sun and the states the planets, repelled yet attracted, and the whole moving regularly and harmoniously in their several orbits."[91] Ancient city-states in Greece had operated under the system of federalism, but it was a unique proposition during the days of the Constitutional Convention.

CONFLICT BETWEEN SMALL AND LARGE STATES

The most contentious issue during the convention proved to be the issue of representation to the legislature. Under the Articles of Confederation, each state, regardless of size, had one vote. The one-state-one-vote clause—Clause V—was written into the Articles of Confederation only after a long and acrimonious battle between the large and small states, and the small states vehemently opposed any plan that would change the current system.

The Virginia Plan recommended proportional representation, in which the number of representatives to the legislature would be based on the size of a state's population. The small states were outraged. "I do not, gentlemen, trust you!"[92] exclaimed Gunning Bedford, a fiery delegate from Delaware. Delaware's instructions, in fact, prohibited its delegates from agreeing to any proposal that

would do away with the one-state-one-vote system. The small states threatened to boycott any union based upon representation according to population.

THE GREAT COMPROMISE

For a while, it looked as though the convention might adjourn without reaching consensus—a prospect the delegates feared. Constantly during the convention, the delegates issued reminders of the threat from abroad. "If we do not come to some agreement among ourselves some foreign sword will probably do the work for us,"[93] warned Elbridge Gerry. Memoirs and correspondence of the delegates reveal how despondent they really were. On July 10, George Washington voiced his concern in a letter to Alexander Hamilton:

> I *almost* despair of seeing a favourable issue to the proceedings of the Convention. . . . I am sorry you went away. I wish you were back. The crisis is equally important and alarming, and no opposition under such circumstances should discourage exertions till the signature is fixed.[94]

In search of a solution, the delegates formed a committee with one representative from each delegation. Led by Roger Sherman, a delegate from Connecticut, the committee drafted a proposal that they hoped would appease both sides. Their solution, which has come to be known as the Great Compromise, is the basis of American government today. In

Delegate Roger Sherman of Connecticut worked hard to resolve the conflict, between large and small states, over representation in the national legislature.

deference to Sherman's influence, the compromise has also been called the Connecticut Compromise.

Sherman's committee proposed a bicameral legislature composed of a House of Representatives and a Senate. The number of each state's members in the House was to depend on the size of its population. The House members were to vote individually and not as state delegations—a provision designed to satisfy the concerns of delegates from larger states. To appease delegates from smaller states, the states would have equal representation in the Senate. Each state would have two senators, serving for six-year terms. Like the representatives, senators would vote individually rather than as a state.

Not everyone agreed right away with the committee's proposal, but a better alternative eluded them. On July 16, the Great Compromise was adopted by a narrow vote of five states to four, thereby ending six weeks of debate and resolving an impasse that had threatened to undermine the work of the convention.

CONFLICT OVER SLAVERY

The Great Compromise was not the only issue that threatened to stall the work of the convention. The delegates also almost came to blows over the issue of slavery.

In the eighteenth century, there were vast differences in the economy, culture, and lifestyle of people in the North and people in the South. In 1787, black Americans constituted almost 20 percent of the American population; 90 percent of these six hundred thousand people were slaves. The economy of the South was based on indigo, rice, and tobacco and completely dependent on the system of slavery.

The issue of slavery pitted the North against the South. Massachusetts was the only one of the thirteen states to outlaw slavery in its constitution, but few slaves lived north of Maryland. Although not able to outlaw slavery completely, some abolitionists believed that they might be able to choke off the slave trade. This was exactly what the southern delegates feared. They viewed this as a threat to their very way of life.

Differences between the northern and the southern states first arose as delegates began to discuss issues related to representation, and disagreement surfaced about how to include slaves in population counts. Southerners wanted to include slaves in the

The issue over whether to count slaves for purposes of determining representation sparked a hostile debate between northern and southern states.

count for representation in the proposed House of Representatives in order to give themselves more representation.

Northerners were appalled. William Paterson of New Jersey put it simply: Slaves were "no free agents, have no personal liberty, no faculty of acquiring property, but on the contrary, are themselves property."[95] Northerners believed that, as property, slaves should not be counted for representation any more than horses or oxen. Antislavery advocates also worried that allowing slaves to be counted for purposes of representation might encourage states to increase their slave populations.

THE THREE-FIFTHS COMPROMISE

Contentious debate over whether or not to count slaves went on for weeks. It became clear that at least two southern states—South Carolina and Georgia—would refuse to sign any constitution that did not sanction slavery. In mid-July, after weeks

of debate, the delegates settled the issue by what became known as the "Three-Fifths Compromise." According to this agreement, slaves would be counted as three-fifths of free persons (five slaves

George Washington hoped that a provision would be included in the Constitution that would legally end slavery.

were counted as three persons) for representation and taxation purposes.

Other clauses regarding slavery were also added during the convention. The delegates agreed to include a provision in the Constitution denying Congress the power to regulate the slave trade before 1808. In addition, northern delegates reluctantly accepted a clause that allowed owners to reclaim fugitive slaves who fled to other states. In return, southern states conceded to allow Congress to impose a tax on each slave.

Not all delegates—or even all southerners—were happy with the conclusion of the debate. George Washington, who himself owned slaves, wrote in a letter to Jefferson that it was his fervent wish "to see some plan adopted by which slavery in this country might be abolished by law."[96]

Washington got his wish, but not for many years. The Civil War would again pit the North against the South in a conflict over slavery. It almost destroyed the union that had been forged tenuously at the Constitutional Convention. The nation survived in part because the framers held resolutely to their belief that a strong union among the states was critical and because they had the foresight to realize that further compromise would be needed in the years to come.

6 The Constitution Is Born

With the great compromises settled in mid-July, the convention had conquered the threat of dissolution, and the delegates could turn their attention to less contentious issues. "So great is the unanimity that prevails in the convention upon all great federal subjects," reported the *Pennsylvania Gazette* on July 18, "that it has been proposed to call the room in which they assemble 'Unanimity Hall.'"[97]

The *Gazette* may have exaggerated, but there was a new feeling of harmony among the delegates. This bode well for the convention. With half the summer gone by there were still a number of issues to be decided. How powerful should the national legislature be? How should the executive branch be structured? Who should have the power for appointing national judges? How would the new nation handle the western territories? And, importantly, what should be the process of ratifying the proposed Constitution, and who should have the power to make it the law of the land?

SEPARATION OF POWERS

The delegates at the Constitutional Convention had one thing in common—they all had lived in the colonies under the rule of England. They had experienced oppression under a tyrannical regime that gave them little or no voice in the decisions that were made. This was foremost in their minds as they developed the Constitution.

The framers of the Constitution wanted to make sure that no one person had as much power as a king. "The accumulation of all powers, legislative, executive, and judiciary, in the same hands," Madison wrote, is the "very definition of tyranny."[98] The framers crafted a system that separated power among three branches of government—the legislative, executive, and judicial.

LEGISLATIVE POWERS

The failure to give sufficient power to Congress had placed the delegates in the position that currently frustrated them. Perhaps the greatest challenge the Union faced under the Articles was the issue of money. Congress was unable to raise funds, which had left the army without much needed supplies during the American Revolution and left Congress without means to pay off its war debts.

But not all the delegates agreed that giving the national legislature the power to raise funds was an appropriate solution. A states' rights advocate to the end, George Mason of Virginia worried that this power might give the national government an excuse to wage war against the states. "Will the militia march from one state to another in order to collect the arrears of taxes from the delinquent members of the Republic?" he asked. "Will not the citizens of the invaded state assist one another till they rise as one man and shake off the Union altogether?"[99]

Practicality won the argument, and Congress's powers were expanded substantially. Madison recommended that Congress be given the power to veto any laws made by states that would interfere with the governance of the nation, but states' rights advocates won that argument. Instead, the delegates decided to list the specific powers granted to Congress. Among these were the powers to regulate trade among the states and with foreign nations, to raise funds through levying taxes and borrowing, to coin money. In addition, Congress was given the power to raise an army and to declare war.

From this dispute over national and state laws, however, came an important development. Surprisingly, it was Luther Martin, who later left the convention in protest, who moved that national laws and treaties "shall be the supreme law of the respective states . . . and that the judiciaries of the several states shall be bound thereby in their decisions, anything in the respective laws of the individual states to the contrary notwithstanding."[100] The del-

egations voted unanimously for what has come to be called the supremacy clause, granting the national government supremacy over state law.

THE EXECUTIVE BRANCH

Thomas Jefferson had said that the lack of an executive under the Articles was

> the source of more evil than we have experienced from any other cause. . . . Nothing is so embarrassing nor so mischievous in a great assembly as the details of execution. The smallest trifle of that kind occupies as long as the most important act of legislation, and takes the place of everything else.[101]

The delegates agreed that an executive branch was needed, but they disagreed about how it should be designed.

The supremacy clause of the Constitution, proposed by Luther Martin, gave federal laws supremacy over state laws.

Charles Pinckney was among the delegates who called for a "vigorous executive."[102] A single vigorous executive, Pinckney's faction argued, was needed to lead the country not just internally but with the kings and queens of Europe. As Alexander Hamilton later wrote in *The Federalist Papers*, a series of articles introducing and defending the Constitution during the struggle for ratification:

Energy in the executive is a leading character in the definition of good government. It is essential to the protection of the community against foreign attacks; it is not less essential to the steady administration of the laws; . . . [or] to the security of liberty against the enterprises and assaults of ambition, of faction, and of anarchy.[103]

Furthermore, explained James Wilson, tyranny could just as easily arise from Congress or the military as from the executive. A strong executive could help protect against the possible oppression of the legislative branch.

Others were vehemently opposed to a single executive because they feared putting too much power in the hands of one person. Benjamin Franklin, for example, advocated having the power of the chief executive vested in three people, each of whom would be drawn from a different section of the country. In the end, this was considered impractical. The delegates decided on a single executive, and after much discussion, decided to call the office the presidency.

The delegates also needed to determine the length of the president's term. Some wanted a life term, but the majority of the delegates agreed that shorter terms would provide the necessary check on the president's powers. After a number of proposals, they settled on four years.

Next, it was necessary to determine how the president was to be elected. James Wilson argued that the president should be elected directly by the people, but even those who thought this was desirable believed that this would not be

Benjamin Franklin suggested that the powers of the president should be vested in three people in order to prevent tyranny.

possible in a country as large as the United States. Communication was slow. How could a person in Georgia know whether a candidate from New York or Massachusetts was well suited for the presidency? Roger Sherman suggested that "the person or persons ought to be appointed by and accountable to the legislature only, which was the depository of the supreme will of the society."[104] However, the delegates remembered their experience under colonial rule, when the governors were at the mercy of the legislatures. Simply put, this would give Congress too much power. If appointed by Congress, "He [the president] will be the mere creature of the Legislature," suggested Gouverneur Morris. "He ought to be elected by the people at large. . . . If the people should elect, they will never fail to prefer some man of distinguished character or services, some man . . . of continental reputation. If the legislature elect, it will be the work of intrigue, of cabal and of faction."[105]

James Wilson was the first delegate to suggest electing a group of people whose only task would be to select the president. The resulting "electoral college" comprises electors chosen by each state legislature. Each state is entitled to a number of electors equal to the total number of senators and representatives it has in the U.S. Congress. Although many critics argue that popular election of the president would be preferable, the electoral college system as described by the framers of the Constitution is still used today to elect the president of the United States.

Gouverneur Morris felt that allowing Congress to choose the president would give the legislative branch too much power.

CHECKS AND BALANCES

The founding fathers were hesitant to vest power in the executive. "Indeed, but for the existence of George Washington, whom everyone trusted and knew would be the first chief executive," postulates historian Forrest McDonald, "the office of president probably would not have been established."[106] As a result, the powers that the delegates granted to the presidency contain strong checks.

Lengthy discussion also centered on the relationship between Congress and the president. Some delegates believed that the president should be given the power to veto laws of Congress. After much discussion, the delegates granted the president the power to veto legislation, but, as an additional check, Congress can overturn a president's veto with a majority two-thirds vote.

FEDERALIST #51

The Federalist Papers *are a series of newspaper articles written by James Madison, Alexander Hamilton, and John Jay under the pen name "Publius" (Latin for "the people") to defend the Constitution during the struggle for ratification. In* Federalist #51, *James Madison defends the principles of separation of powers and republican processes. The following excerpt describes the fundamental basis of the system of checks and balances put forth in the Constitution.*

"[T]he great security against a gradual concentration of the several powers in the same department consists in giving to those who administer each department the necessary constitutional means and personal motives to resist encroachments of the others. The provision for defense must in this, as in all other cases, be made commensurate to the danger of attack. Ambition must be made to counteract ambition. The interest of the man must be connected with the constitutional rights of the place.

It may be a reflection on human nature that such devices should be necessary to control the abuses of government. But what is government itself but the greatest of all reflections on human nature? If men were angels, no government would be necessary. If angels were to govern men, neither external nor internal controls on government would be necessary. In framing a government which is to be administered by men over men, the great difficulty lies in this: you must first enable the government to control the governed; and in the next place oblige it to control itself. A dependence on the people is, no doubt, the primary control on the government; but experience has taught mankind the necessity of auxiliary precautions."

A final check on the president's power is the process of impeachment and removal from office. Some delegates argued against impeachment because they believed it was a threat to the power of the presidency itself to serve as a check on the actions of Congress. In the end, the delegates agreed that there were circumstances, which they vaguely termed "high crimes and misdemeanors," that could merit a president's removal from office. Two presidents have been impeached—Andrew Johnson in 1868 and Bill Clinton in 1999—but neither was removed from office. Debate over what specific actions qualify as a high crime or misdemeanor continued throughout President Clinton's impeachment hearings.

THE JUDICIAL BRANCH

Fewer discussions took place regarding the judiciary than either of the other two branches. The delegates quickly agreed to create a supreme court, give judges life tenure, and pay them a salary. As with the president, there was initial disagreement over how justices should be chosen. James Wilson opposed congressional selection, arguing that "experience showed the impropriety of such appointments by numerous bodies. Intrigue, partiality, and concealment were the necessary consequences."[107] Others, however, including John Rutledge of South Carolina, were "by no means disposed to grant so great a power to any single person [the president]. The people will think we are leaning too much towards Monarchy."[108] In the end, they agreed that the president would nominate the justices and the Senate would confirm their appointment. Like other measures, this is part of the elaborate system of checks and balances the delegates crafted.

To resolve some of the problems encountered under the Articles of Confederation, the delegates endowed the judicial branch the power to resolve disputes among the states. No longer would the Union be at the mercy of bickering among states over borders, interstate trade, or other issues that had previously plagued it. Interestingly, most of the details regarding how the judiciary branch should conduct itself were left out of the written Constitution.

THE WEST

At the time of the Constitutional Convention, the territory owned by the thirteen states included but a fraction of the total area of the United States today. Much of the land to the west of the Appalachian Mountains was unexplored wilderness.

However, the delegates could foresee vast changes coming. Settlers were moving west in hordes, occupying the untamed land. By 1790, the people migrating over the Appalachian Mountains numbered more than 110,000. Another 20,000 migrants were moving west via flatboats on the Ohio River. What would happen when these new areas were settled? How should new states be admitted into the Union?

The convention looked for inspiration to the Northwest Ordinance, which had been drafted by Massachusetts delegate Rufus King. The ordinance provided a formula for dividing the Northwest Territory into three to five areas, provided for an interim government, and spelled out how each area could become a state and join the Union when it reached sixty thousand inhabitants.

Worried about creating another monarchy, John Rutledge sought to limit the powers of the president.

Under the terms of the Northwest Ordinance, new states were to be admitted on an equal footing with existing states, but some delegates argued against giving future states equal power. They not only feared a shift in political power but argued that the states would consist primarily of mostly poor, start-up farmers, which would "drain our wealth into the Western country."[109]

Would conditional acceptance into the Union be a solution? No, argued James Madison and George Mason. The West "neither would nor ought to submit to a Union which degraded them from an equal rank with other states. . . . If the Western States hereafter arising should be admitted into the Union, they ought to be considered as equals and as brethren."[110] Roger Sherman pointed out that the West was not so different from the existing states and cautioned, "We are providing for our posterity, for our children and our grandchildren, who would be as likely to be citizens of new Western states as of the old states."[111]

At the time for the final vote, most of the delegates agreed that states "should be admitted on the same terms with the original states,"[112] but Gouverneur Morris was able to get the clause guaranteeing this right struck from the Constitution. Thus, in the end, the Constitution left to Congress the power to decide how states would be admitted. All thirty-seven states that have joined the nation since 1787 have been admitted on equal footing. Americans may take this for granted today, but historian Catherine Drinker Bowen reminds us of what might have happened:

[I]f the Convention had failed, if the Western Territory had not been admitted on terms of equality, there might have followed a whole series of revolutions, of civil strife and territorial secession as the nation pushed ever farther westward and new states reached maturity. Under such conditions it is not impossible to conceive

Delegates had to decide when the growing western territories should become states.

of the United States proper as ending at the Appalachian Ridge.[113]

WHO SHALL RATIFY?

The process to be implemented to approve the draft constitution as the governing document for the new United States still needed to be decided. The original Virginia Plan had proposed that ratification "after the approbation of Congress" should be decided by "an assembly or assemblies of Representatives, recommended by the several Legislatures to be expressly chosen by the people."[114] Although the Committee of the Whole had approved this at the outset of the convention, when the plan came up for debate later, some delegates voiced their opposition. It was impractical; there was no system in place in most states for such assemblies to be chosen. The state legislatures were the appropriate parties for approving the new constitution, they explained.

James Madison believed that popular ratification was the key to acceptance of the new constitution. He argued that the people were "the fountain of all power [and] could alter constitutions as they pleased."[115] Further, there was a great difference between a mere confederation and the system the delegates were now creating. "The difference between a system founded on the legislatures only and one founded on the people [is] the true difference between a *league* or *treaty,* and a *Constitution.*"[116] The latter idea was clearly preferable because it would better protect the rights of the people. "A law violating a constitution established by the people themselves would be considered by the judges as null and void."[117]

The delegates discussed the possibility of further debating the Constitution in the state legislatures and then holding a second convention. The convention cringed. It had taken years to get Congress to call for this convention; the chances that another opportunity might present itself were slim. Others argued that the delegates were bound to follow the ratification process established by the Articles of Confederation. This meant that state legislatures had the power to ratify—or not to ratify. It further meant that approval was needed by all thirteen states before the Constitution would go into effect.

The delegates were appalled. They believed that using the ratification process spelled out by the Articles would mean the death of the Constitution. James Wilson declared, "After spending four or five months in the laborious and arduous task of forming a government of our country, we are ourselves at the close throwing insuperable obstacles in the way of its success."[118] The delegates fully expected resistance from several states, including Rhode Island, which had even declined to send delegates to the meeting. Nathaniel Gorham of Massachusetts asked, "Will anyone say that all the states are to suffer themselves to be ruined if Rhode Island should persist in her opposition to general measures?"[119]

The delegates defeated the proposal to give state legislatures the power to ratify. Instead, by a vote of nine to one, they passed a resolution "to refer the Constitution, after the appropriation of Congress, to assemblies chosen by the people."[120]

The delegates also agreed that the Constitution would go into effect after nine of the thirteen states ratified it. For those nine states, the Constitution would become a binding document and the supreme law of the land. Other states could decide independently whether or not to join the union. The ratification process thereby ensured that each state committed itself to the principles of the Constitution.

"WE, THE PEOPLE"

At the end of the Constitutional Convention, the delegates voted to entrust all they had accomplished to a committee led Gouverneur Morris to put it in clearly written form. Among the changes that Morris's committee made was one that changed the very nature of the document. The committee changed the first line from "We, the people of the States of North Carolina, Virginia, Massachusetts, [etc.]" to "We, the people of the United States." With this stroke of the pen, the Constitution was no longer a contract among states but among the people.

As Morris wrote in the Preamble to the Constitution, the citizenry of the United States needed a written constitution "in order to form a more perfect Union, establish justice, insure domestic tranquility, provide for the common defense, promote the general welfare, and secure the blessings of liberty to ourselves and our posterity." Although the Constitution was yet to be tested, the framers knew that to accomplish these purposes, the Constitution would need to balance the interests of various parties and be able to adapt to changing circumstances.

THE DELEGATES AFFIX THEIR SIGNATURES

Alexander Hamilton was among those who believed that it was critical that the delegations present a united front in signing the document. In a letter to James Madison, Hamilton cautioned, "A few characters of consequence, by opposing or even refusing to sign the Constitution, might do infinite mischief by kindling the latent sparks which lurk under an enthusiasm in favor of the Convention which may soon subside."[121]

Benjamin Franklin had written a speech encouraging the delegates to put their names on the Constitution, which James Wilson now read aloud. Although he recognized that the Constitution had flaws, Franklin expressed his doubt that the convention could do better and cautioned against holding out for a truly perfect document. When Wilson finished, Franklin moved that the Constitution be signed.

Several delegates who had opposed a united government had returned home. Only three of the delegates who remained at the convention on September 17—Edmund Randolph, Elbridge Gerry, and George Mason—refused to sign the document. Randolph withheld his signature because he wanted to leave himself free to decide on the merit of the document during Virginia's ratification process. "He apologized for his refusing to sign the Constitution," wrote Madison in his record of the proceedings. "He said . . . that he did not mean by this refusal to decide that he should oppose the Constitution [outside of the convention]. He meant only to keep himself free to be governed by his duty as it should be prescribed by his future judgment."[122]

Elbridge Gerry declined to sign the document because he advocated more moderate change. Perhaps with Shays's Rebellion in mind, he expressed concern that the proposed constitution might provoke civil war between supporters of a strong government and those who feared it. George Mason refused his signature on account of the lack of a bill of rights. He argued that without such a bill, the Constitution threatened individual rights and liberties. Many people joined Mason in successfully lobbying for a bill of rights during the ratification process. The addition of a bill of rights was to be the first change made to the Constitution.

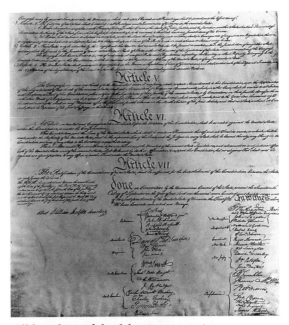

All but three of the delegates present on September 17, 1787, signed the final draft of the Constitution.

A RISING SUN

Benjamin Franklin had been relatively silent during the convention. At eighty-one, he was in poor health and needed to be carried to and from Independence Hall. He was perhaps the most revered American save George Washington, known not just as a statesman, but as a scientist, printer, and philanthropist. He was proud of what the convention had accomplished and optimistic about the Constitution's promise. In his notes of the meeting, James Madison wrote,

> Whilst the last members were signing it [the Constitution] Dr. Franklin looking towards the President's Chair, at the back of which a rising sun happened to be painted, observed to a few members near him, that Painters had found it difficult to distinguish in their art a rising from a setting sun. "I have" said he, "often and often in the course of the Session, and the vicissitudes of my hopes and fears as to its issue, looked at that behind the President without being able to tell whether it was rising or setting; but now at length I have the happiness to know that it is a rising and not a setting Sun."[123]

On this positive note, this historic meeting of some of the greatest American minds adjourned. The Constitution was now in the hands of Congress and the people.

7 The Struggle for Ratification

The delegates had signed the Constitution, but it was by no means assured that Congress or the state legislatures would accept it. "The moment this plan goes forth," said Gouverneur Morris at the end of the convention, "all other considerations will be laid aside—and the great question will be, shall there be a national government or not? And this must take place or a general anarchy will be the alternative."[124]

The ensuing public discussion about the Constitution and the ratification conventions were characterized by spirited debate and vehemently fought arguments. Seven times Rhode Island voted against sending the document to a state convention for ratification, and North Carolina rejected the Constitution at its first ratification convention in August 1788. The delegates at the Massachusetts referendum narrowly approved ratification by a vote of 187 to 168, and they proposed amendments to correct perceived defects. Several states followed suit and agreed to ratify the document only with strings attached.

The Constitution was a radical departure from previous forms of government. Just as the delegates were wary of giving too much power to the national government, so too were the people. They had fought and survived a bloody and expensive war to throw off the shackles of tyranny—would they put their faith in a new regime? As John Marshall, who would become chief justice of the Supreme Court, explained,

> In some of the adopting states a majority of the people were in the opposition. In all of them, the numerous amendments which were proposed demonstrate the reluctance with which the new government was accepted; and that a dread of dismemberment, not an approbation of the particular system under consideration, had induced an acquiescence in it.[125]

Benjamin Franklin counseled advocates of the Constitution to work hard to change minds. "To get the bad customs of a country changed and new ones, though better, introduced, it is necessary first to remove the prejudices of the people, enlighten their ignorance, and convince them that their interests will be promoted by the proposed changes; and this is not the work of a day."[126] And so the contest began.

John Marshall noted the reluctance of the nation's citizens to place their trust in a new form of government.

ON TO CONGRESS

Accompanying the official copy of the Constitution delivered to Congress in New York was a letter from George Washington. The letter emphasized the spirit of collaboration and compromise with which the Constitution was written:

> That it will meet the full and entire approbation of every state is not perhaps to be expected; but each will doubtless consider, that had her interest alone been consulted, the consequences might have been particularly disagreeable or injurious to others; that it is liable to as few exceptions as could reasonably have been expected, we hope and believe; that it may promote lasting welfare of that country

so dear to us all, and secure her freedom and happiness, is our ardent wish.[127]

The Constitution was often initially met with skepticism. Some people feared that it took power out of the hands of the many and put it into the hands of a few. "It cannot be denied, with truth," claimed Richard Henry Lee of Virginia before the Congress, "that this new Constitution is, in its first principles, highly and dangerously oligarchic; and it is a point agreed, that a government of the few is, of all governments, the worst."[128] Opponents also criticized the Constitution's lack of a guarantee of rights or personal liberty. The only members of Congress who raised objections, however, were from the states of New York and Virginia.

In part this was due to the fact that the congressmen who had served as delegates had returned to New York to see to it that the Constitution was approved. Of the thirty representatives present at the discussions in Congress, ten had been members of the Constitutional Convention. As a result of their influence, Congress acted quickly to approve the Constitution. After only a few days of debate, the Constitution was sent on to the states.

THE BATTLE OF WORDS

When the Constitution was made public, it raised much fervent discussion and debate, often mimicking the debates at the Constitutional Convention. James Madison wrote to Thomas Jefferson that the Constitution occupied "almost the whole political attention of America."[129] Newspapers everywhere published the Constitution as soon as they received it and ran commentaries with arguments for and against ratification. The argument between the Federalists, who approved of the Constitution, and the Antifederalists, who opposed it, raged in the public eye for months.

George Washington recognized that the struggle for ratification would be fought in the press. "Much will depend . . . on literary abilities," he wrote to a colleague upon returning to his home in Mount Vernon, "and the recommendation of it [the Constitution] by good pens, should it be openly [and] publicly attacked in the Gazettes."[130]

SUPPORT FOR THE CONSTITUTION

Supporters of a strong national government, including many of the men who had attended the Constitutional Convention, rallied around the Constitution and lobbied hard in states where ratification hung in the balance. Among the most strident defenses of the Constitution was *The Federalist Papers*, a series of eighty-five essays written by Alexander Hamilton, James Madison, and John Jay, and published under the pen name "Publius." Written primarily to persuade New York to ratify the document, *The Federalist Papers* remains a brilliant and comprehensive explanation of the principles and beliefs underlying the Constitution.

"THERE IS NO ALTERNATIVE"

George Washington continued to lobby strongly for the Constitution. He believed that the alternative was anarchy, as he expresses in a letter written December 14, 1787. This excerpt is reprinted from Historical Moments: Changing Interpretations of America's Past, *by Jim R. McClellan.*

"My decided opinion on the matter is, that there is no alternative between the adoption of it and anarchy. . . . All the opposition to it that I have yet seen is addressed more to the passions than to reason. General government is now suspended by a thread; I might go further and say it is really at an end. . . .

The Constitution that is submitted, is not free from imperfections; but there are as few radical defects in it as could well be expected, considering the heterogeneous mass of which the Convention was composed—and the diversity of interests which were to be reconciled. A Constitutional door being opened, for future alterations and amendments, I think it would be wise in the People to adopt what is offered to them; and I wish it may be by as great a majority of them as in the body that decided on it."

John Adams, who also had been representing America in Europe during the Constitutional Convention, wrote home his opinion. Adams had studied systems of government and had written a book about government, which had been passed around Philadelphia as the delegates completed their work. In his assessment of the Constitution,

> The public mind cannot be occupied about a nobler object than the proposed plan of government. It appears to be admirably calculated to cement all America in affection and interest as one great nation. A result of compromise cannot perfectly coincide with every one's ideas of perfection; but, as all the great principles necessary to order, liberty, and safety are respected in it, and provision made for amendments as they be found necessary, I hope to hear of its adoption by all the states.[131]

THE OPPOSITION MOUNTS ITS CASE

Those who opposed ratification of the Constitution were equally active penning editorials for local newspapers as those who supported it. Upon returning home after the convention, Elbridge Gerry, who had refused to sign the Constitution, printed a long list of criticisms of the Constitution. Richard Henry Lee of Virginia spelled out his objections in a widely read pamphlet that he called *Letters of the Federal Farmer*. Governor George Clinton of New York, who had for some time fought

New York governor George Clinton publicly attacked the Constitution and wrote newspaper articles in which he opposed its ratification.

against the formation of a strong central government (hence the appointment of Antifederalists to the state's delegation to the Constitutional Convention), wrote a series of newspaper articles in opposition to ratification, which he signed "Cato."

The Antifederalists mounted criticism on a number of fronts. Many people, particularly farmers in rural areas, feared that a central government would be insensitive to local issues and concerns. Led by Patrick Henry and other respected statesmen, states' rights advocates argued that a strong national government would annihilate the states and quash the rights of the people. Both rich and poor expressed concerns that the government would "fall into the hands of the few and the great."[132] In addition, citizens in Rhode Island, whose economy was thriving, feared that a new system for issuing money would cut into their prosperity.

Recognizing that the people were justifiably wary of giving too much power to a new government, some Antifederalists played on the suspicions of the people. "The evil genius of darkness presided at the Constitution's birth. It came forth under the veil of mystery,"[133] wrote one editorial. Mercy Otis Warren, author of the first history of the American Revolution to be published in America, said that the Constitution was the result of "dark, secret and profound intrigues" of "rapacious" men.[134]

There were numerous other criticisms: The executive was too powerful; the slavery clauses were immoral; the convention itself was illegal. People were suspicious of the intentions of the convention delegates. They worried that the seat of the national government would be a fortified town occupied by a standing army, ready to run rampant over the rights of the citizens. They also feared the national government's power of taxation. "Does not this Constitution take away all we have—all our property?" asked a delegate to the Massachusetts ratification convention. "Does it not lay all taxes, duties, imposts, and excises? And what more have we to give?"[135]

THE CLAMOR FOR A BILL OF RIGHTS

Perhaps the strongest criticism of the Constitution was its lack of a declaration of rights. The oppression that had taken place under British rule was still fresh in the minds of Americans when the Consti-

tution was made public in 1787. Many people agreed with George Mason that approval should be denied until such a bill was added. In a letter from France, Thomas Jefferson outlined how he would address the problem:

> I would advocate [the Constitution] warmly till nine should have adopted, & then as warmly take the other side to convince the remaining four that they ought not to come into it till the declaration of rights is annexed to it. By this means we should secure all the good of it, & procure so respectable an opposition as would induce the accepting states to offer a bill of rights. This would be the happiest turn the thing could take.[136]

The delegates at the convention had not been against the rights of the people. Rather they believed that a bill of rights was unnecessary. "Why declare that things shall not be done which there is no power to do?"[137] asked Alexander Hamilton. Furthermore, each of the state constitutions had bills of rights that would still be in effect under the new system of government. Some people also worried that listing rights that were to be protected would endanger any rights not listed. "Enumerate all the rights of men?" asked James Wilson. "I am sure that no gentleman in the late Convention would have attempted such a thing."[138]

When the Federalists realized that the issue of the bill of rights would be a sticking point for ratification in many states, they generally conceded that one should be added.

In Jefferson's Opinion

Throughout the Constitutional Convention, Thomas Jefferson corresponded from Paris with a number of the delegates. In a letter written to James Madison on December 20, 1787, Jefferson gives his reactions to the Constitution. Jefferson highlights the elements that he believes to be particularly beneficial in the Constitution, but he laments the lack of a bill of rights. This excerpt is taken from Thomas Jefferson's Writings, *a Library of America publication.*

"I like much the general idea of framing a government which should go on itself peaceably, without needing continual recurrence to the state legislatures. I like the organization of the government into Legislative, Judiciary & Executive. I like the power given to the Legislature to levy taxes; and for that reason solely approve of the greater house being chosen by the people directly. For tho' I think a house chosen by them will be very illy qualified to legislate for the Union, for foreign nations etc., yet this evil does not weigh against the good of preserving inviolate the fundamental principle that people are not to be taxed but by the representatives chosen immediately by themselves. I am captivated by the compromise of the opposite claims of the great & little states, of the latter to equal, and former to proportional influence. I am much pleased too with the substitution of the method of voting by persons, instead of that of voting by states, and I like the negative given to the Executive with a third of either house, though I should have liked it better had the Judiciary been associated for that purpose, or invested with a similar and separate power. . . .

I will now add what I do not like. First the omission of a bill of rights providing clearly . . . for freedom of religion, freedom of the press, protection against standing armies, restriction against monopolies, the eternal and unremitting force of the habeas corpus laws, and trials by jury in all matters of fact triable by the laws of the land and not by the law of nations. . . .

The second feature I dislike, and greatly dislike, is the abandonment in every instance of the necessity of rotation in office and most particularly in the case of the president. Experience concurs with reason in concluding that the first magistrate will always be re-elected if the Constitution permits it. He is then an officer for life. . . .

I own I am not a friend to a very energetic government. It is always oppressive. The late rebellion in Massachusetts has given more alarm than I think it should have done. . . . No country should be so long without [a rebellion]. Nor will any degree of power in the hands of government prevent insurrections."

PENNSYLVANIA RUSHES TO JUDGMENT

Usually the battle over ratification was fought with words. But occasionally, the dispute became violent. Open debates became riots or brawls. Some people tried to settle the issue in duels. In Pennsylvania, pandemonium erupted even as the legislature made a motion to appoint delegates to a state ratification convention.

Pennsylvania's pro-Constitution assembly hurried to hold the ratification convention. The convention opened at the Philadelphia State House on November 21. Day after day, James Wilson was on his feet commending the Constitution and explaining its virtues to the sixty-nine convention delegates. Central to his argument was the explanation that a strong government was needed to pay off America's war debts and negotiate trade agreements with European nations. Many of the delegates from rural counties who had planned to vote against the Constitution were persuaded to change their minds. On December 12, after weeks of speeches, Pennsylvania ratified the governing document by a vote of forty-six to twenty-three.

Wilson intended to make a speech during the celebration that followed, but just as he began, he was attacked by an angry mob of Antifederalists. It was said later that Wilson would have been killed had not an old soldier thrown himself over the fallen man and taken the blows.

THE FIRST STATES TO RATIFY

Despite its haste, Pennsylvania did not have the honor of being the first state to ratify. That honor went to the small state of Delaware, which unanimously approved the document in December 1787, four days before Pennsylvania's vote took place. A week later, New Jersey also approved the document with a unanimous vote. Georgia and Connecticut quickly followed suit, ratifying in early January 1788.

These relatively small states saw the benefit of joining together, particularly since Pennsylvania was onboard. Both New Jersey and Connecticut, which had for quite some time been hampered by import duties levied by New York, needed protection from what Oliver Ellsworth, a delegate at the Constitutional Convention, called "the rapacity and ambition of New York."[139] Georgia also hoped to gain additional strength from the national government in protecting its frontier. As George Washington had written of Georgia, "If a weak state with Indians on its back and the Spaniards on its flank does not see the necessity of a General Government, there must I think be wickedness of insanity in the way."[140]

MASSACHUSETTS HOLDS ITS CONVENTION

Things did not go so smoothly for the Federalists in Massachusetts. True to the state's democratic spirit and town meeting history, 355 delegates were elected to its ratification convention in January 1788. Twenty-one of the delegates had participated in Shays's Rebellion, and most of the delegates from the western rural counties agreed with these delegates that it was unwise to give the power of taxation to a national government. The Federalists estimated that at least two hundred of the delegates were not in favor of the Constitution. Samuel Adams, an aging firebrand of the Revolution, stood among them.

While they may have been a minority, the Federalists at the Massachusetts ratification convention were strong leaders who were known and respected throughout the state. Rufus King, a member of the Constitutional Convention, was among those who were staunchly committed to getting enough votes for ratification.

The Federalists countered the Antifederalists' cry for a bill of rights with a suggestion: Ratify the Constitution as it is now, and we will join with you in making sure that the guarantees you seek are added through amendment. The Federalists drafted a series of possible amendments. Because they believed that the Antifederalist faction of the convention would be more willing to agree to the plan if it came from one of their own, they asked John Hancock, a wealthy signer of the Declaration who had made known his sentiments against the Constitution, to present it.

The persuasion and cunning of the Federalists, as well as the motion to attach stipulated amendments, proved effective. On February 6, 1788, by a close vote (187 to 168), Massachusetts became the sixth state to ratify the Constitution.

THE CONSTITUTION TAKES EFFECT

More states held conventions in the spring of 1788. In April and May, Maryland and

Samuel Adams was among the many individuals in Massachusetts who opposed the ratification of the Constitution.

South Carolina both voted for ratification by healthy margins.

New Hampshire had difficulty deciding. After adjourning once without voting, the convention met again. In addition to the usual arguments against the Constitution, some New Hampshirites mounted opposition because the Constitution failed to outlaw slavery. But on June 21, 1788, New Hampshire became the ninth state to ratify, narrowly defeating the opponents fifty-seven to forty-seven. With the vote for ratification in New Hampshire, the Constitution went into effect and the Union was established.

However, the Federalists were still worried. Two of the biggest and most powerful states—Virginia and New York—were

"THEY WILL SWALLOW UP US"

Massachusetts held the largest ratification convention. There, as elsewhere, the debates often became heated. Here, Amos Singletary, a farmer who had lived through the American Revolution, speaks out against the Constitution. His mistrust of those who favored the Constitution is evident in this excerpt from The Spirit of 1787 *by Milton Lomask.*

"Some gentlemen have called on them that were on the stage in the beginning of our troubles, in the year 1775. I was one of them. And I say that if anybody had proposed such a Constitution as this in that day, it would have been thrown away at once. It would not have been looked at. . . . Does not this Constitution take away all we have—all our property? Does it not lay all taxes, duties, imposts, and excises? And what more have we to give? . . .

These lawyers and men of learning, and moneyed men that talk so finely, and gloss over matters too smoothly, to make us poor illiterate people swallow down the pill, expect to get into Congress themselves. They expect to be the managers of this Constitution, and get all the power and all the money into their own hands. And then they will swallow up us little fellows . . . just as the whale swallowed up Jonah."

not part of the Union. How long could the Union last without the endorsement of these states? America's eyes turned to the ratification conventions underway in these two states.

THE VIRGINIA CONVENTION

During the ratification process, Virginia, which still included areas that are now West Virginia and Kentucky, was the largest state in the Union. One-fifth of all the inhabitants of America lived in Virginia. In Virginia, as had been the case in Massachusetts, the Federalists believed that more than half of the delegates were against ratification. Furthermore, the Antifederalists had articulate and powerful leaders, many of whom were well known and respected for the role they had played in the American Revolution. George Mason, Patrick Henry, Richard Henry Lee—heroes of the Revolution all—were in opposition to the Constitution, particularly lamenting its lack of a bill of rights. "I need not take pains to show, that the principles of this system, are extremely pernicious, impolitic, and dangerous," declared Patrick Henry at the outset of the ratification convention. "The rights of conscience, trial by jury, liberty of the press, all your immunities and franchises, all pretensions of human rights and privileges, are rendered insecure, if not lost, by this change."[141]

But the Federalists were also a powerful lot. In addition to James Madison, proponents included Edmund Pendleton, the state's supreme court judge; George Wythe, a lawyer and educator who had also been a delegate at the Constitutional Convention; John Marshall, a young lawyer who would later become chief justice of the Supreme Court; and George Nicholas, a lawyer with a silver tongue that could hold audiences in rapt attention for hours.

The Federalists hammered home the inadequacies of the Articles. "What was the situation of this country before the meeting of the federal Convention?" asked Pendleton. "Our general government was totally inadequate to the purpose of its institution; our commerce decayed; our finances deranged; public and private credit destroyed."[142] To the cry that there existed no formal bill of rights, the Federalists argued, "There is no quarrel between government and liberty. The former is the shield and protector of the latter."[143] Only a strong national government could protect the states from fighting with one another and from insurrections within them. Furthermore, argued the Federalists, the Constitution gave the people the power to correct it. "The people made the Constitution, and the people can unmake it," later

RATIFICATION BY THE STATE CONVENTIONS

State	Date of Approval	Yes	No
Delaware	December 7, 1787	30	0
Pennsylvania	December 12, 1787	46	23
New Jersey	December 18, 1787	38	0
Georgia	January 2, 1788	26	0
Connecticut	January 9, 1788	128	40
Massachusetts	February 6, 1788	187	168
Maryland	April 26, 1788	63	11
South Carolina	May 23, 1788	149	73
New Hampshire	June 21, 1788	57	47
Virginia	June 25, 1788	89	79
New York	July 26, 1788	30	27
North Carolina	November 21, 1789	194	77
Rhode Island	May 29, 1790	34	32

Source: McClellan, *Historical Moments*, p. 144.

wrote John Marshall in the case of *Cohen v. Virginia*.

After weeks of heated, often contentious debate, George Wythe moved that the Constitution be adopted with subsequent amendments that would spell out the rights the Antifederalists so fervently desired. As debate continued into the next day, James Madison promised the convention that he would work for a bill of rights if the Constitution were adopted. Apparently, the delegates took him at his word. About an hour later, the Constitution was ratified by a vote of eighty-nine to seventy-nine.

NEW YORK RELUCTANTLY RATIFIES

When New York's sixty-five delegates met in Poughkeepsie on June 17, the An-

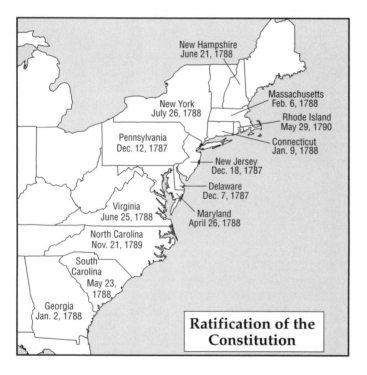

New Hampshire
June 21, 1788

Massachusetts
Feb. 6, 1788

New York
July 26, 1788

Rhode Island
May 29, 1790

Pennsylvania
Dec. 12, 1787

Connecticut
Jan. 9, 1788

New Jersey
Dec. 18, 1787

Delaware
Dec. 7, 1787

Virginia
June 25, 1788

Maryland
April 26, 1788

North Carolina
Nov. 21, 1789

South
Carolina
May 23,
1788

Georgia
Jan. 2, 1788

Ratification of the Constitution

tifederalist majority was overwhelming. Beyond the outskirts of New York City, the Constitution had few advocates. Under the current system, New Yorkers paid little or no taxes because the state was able to generate needed revenue by placing duties on imported items entering New York Harbor. The Antifederalists were led by George Clinton, a savvy politician who would serve as New York's governor for more than twenty years.

The argument in New York was similar to that in Virginia. Under one of the provisions, the Constitution would not be allowed to take effect until after the holding of a second federal convention at which a series of amendments would be developed. Word of New Hampshire's ratification making adoption of the Constitution official did not faze the New York convention. They believed that no Union could function without the help of Virginia.

However, the Federalists had on their side two powerful forces: Alexander Hamilton and the state of Virginia. Hamilton used every weapon in his power to convince the convention that its fears were unfounded. He went through the Constitution clause by clause, pointing out how the convention had adequately addressed their concerns.

The other weapon lay outside of the state. One of the arguments that the New York delegates made at the convention was that no union could survive without the cooperation of powerful Vir-

A crowd celebrates the adoption of the U.S. Constitution.

ginia. Thus, the delegates meeting in New York anxiously awaited news of the Virginia convention. When they learned that Virginia had voted in favor of ratification, their opposition wavered.

Recognizing that they would be powerless against a union that included Virginia, Hamilton again pressed for ratification. What would become of New York if it resisted joining this increasingly powerful alliance? How could it survive? Melancton Smith, a wealthy Antifederalist, admitted later that he was influenced by some of Hamilton's arguments. On July 24, he moved that the delegates endorse the Constitution as written. On July 26, 1788, by a narrow vote of thirty to twenty-seven, New York became the eleventh state to join the Union.

"'TIS DONE"

Everyone assumed that the other two states would soon follow suit. With the Union guaranteed, it was in no state's best interest to decline to join. After two difficult conventions in which ratification failed, North Carolina voted for ratification on November 21, 1789. And, in May 1790, more than a year after George Washington took office as the first president, Rhode Island grudgingly became the last of the original thirteen states to ratify the Constitution.

Celebrations erupted throughout the new nation in support of its new Constitution. People thronged the streets to watch "federal processions." On July 4, 1788, Philadelphia staged a lavish parade. Marching bands and citizens joined together in a new celebratory song that Francis Hopkinson, a Pennsylvania delegate to the Constitutional Convention, had written for the occasion:

> Hail to this festival!—all hail the day! Columbia's standard on her roof display! And let the people's motto ever be, United thus, and thus united, free![144]

"'Tis done," said Benjamin Rush, a speaker at the happy occasion. "We have become a nation!"[145]

Chapter

8 An Enduring Legacy

The story of the U.S. Constitution did not end with its ratification. Since the adoption of the Constitution, it has continued to develop—to change and to grow and to govern a nation that has gone through vast changes. For this reason, it has been called a living document.

The U.S. Constitution commanded great admiration when it was written. As the Constitutional Convention adjourned, George Washington declared that the Constitution was "much to be wondered at . . . a little short of a miracle."[146] Charles Pinckney of South Carolina told his colleagues that they should be "astonishingly pleased" that a government "so perfect could have been formed from such discordant and unpromising material."[147]

Yet, the Constitution, as conceived of by the delegates at the convention, has been proved to be far from perfect. "Few features of the Constitution functioned as written," write historians Oscar and Lillian Handlin. "The federal and state constitutions endured not through perfection as composed but through practical flexibility; government and governed improvised as needed."[148]

The founding fathers realized that their document was not perfect and that inter-

pretation would play a role. When a friend complimented Gouverneur Morris on the fine Constitution he and his colleagues had written, Morris replied, "That depends on how it is construed."[149]

The real strength of the U.S. Constitution is its flexibility. In their wisdom, the founding fathers left open the door of amendment—a way to change the system peaceably and without revolution. Furthermore, by writing the document as a statement of broad principles rather than a list of specific actions and activities for which the government would be responsible, the framers of the Constitution enabled later generations to interpret the document in the context of their times. This flexibility has vastly contributed to the staying power of the document.

A GOOD CANVAS MADE BETTER

The framers of the Constitution recognized the importance of developing a document with an eye toward the future. "We should consider," said James Wilson, "that we are providing a Constitution for future generations and not merely for the circumstances of the moment."[150] Throughout

George Washington taking the oath of office to become the first president of the United States.

his correspondence following the Constitutional Convention, George Washington reminded people of their ability to change the document in accordance with their wishes. In a letter written during the struggle for ratification, he wrote:

> I saw the imperfections of the constitution I aided in the birth of, before it was handed to the public; but I am fully persuaded it is the best that can be obtained at this time, that it is free from the imperfections with which it is charged, and that it or disunion is before us to choose from. If the first is our election, when the defects of it are experienced, a constitutional door is opened for amendments and may be adopted in a peaceable manner, without tumult or disorder.[151]

Thomas Jefferson referred to the Constitution as "a good canvas, on which some strokes only want retouching."[152] In

1803, he admonished his fellow countrymen, "Let us go on perfecting the Constitution by adding, by way of amendment, those forms which time and trial show are still wanting."[153]

Recognizing that the document was not perfect, the founding fathers had the wisdom to incorporate into the document a way to change it without negating the fundamental principles on which it is based. Since it was created in 1787, the Constitution has been changed twenty-seven times through the addition of constitutional amendments.

THE DAWN OF A NEW DAY

On April 16, 1789, George Washington again stepped out of retirement to answer his country's call. Two days earlier, Charles Thomson, the secretary of Congress, had ridden to Mount Vernon to inform Washington that he had been elected the first president of the United States:

> I have now, sir to inform you that the proofs you have given of your patriotism and of your readiness to sacrifice domestic separation and private enjoyments to preserve the liberty and promote the happiness of your country did not permit the two Houses [of Congress] to harbour a doubt of your undertaking this great, this important office to which you are called not only by the unanimous vote of the electors, but by the voice of America.[154]

Little was certain as Washington left for New York, the temporary seat of the government. The government had no permanent location and no plan of action. North Carolina and Rhode Island were not even part of the Union at this time. "We are in a wilderness without a single footstep to guide us,"[155] wrote James Madison, who had been elected to the nation's first Congress. Washington also recognized that he walked "on untrodden ground." "There is scarcely any part of my conduct which may not hereafter be drawn into precedent,"[156] he wrote. But the founding fathers expected things to improve. "Our successors will have an easier task, and by degrees the way will become smooth, short, and certain."[157]

During this first administration, the executive branch and Congress struggled together to learn how to best work together. Above all, they endeavored to ensure that the new system would not fail.

A Promise and a Proposal

Among the first orders of business was to appease the Antifederalists by fulfilling the promise to rectify what they saw as a major flaw of the Constitution—the lack of a bill of rights. In his first inaugural address, Washington urged representatives of Congress to propose amendments that showed "a reverence for the characteristic rights of freemen and a regard for public harmony."[158] On June 8, 1789, just weeks after he had joined the first Congress, James Madison lived up to his promise and made a motion that Congress begin the amendment process for adding a bill of rights.

There was already a long list of rights that had been suggested. The ratification conventions of Massachusetts, South Carolina, New Hampshire, Virginia, and New York had formally proposed various bill of rights amendments; together these numbered more than two hundred. Many of these amendments duplicated one another, but even when combined, almost a hundred different changes had been recommended. Madison encapsulated the most important ideas and ideals in seventeen proposals, including the ten amendments that would become the U.S. Bill of Rights. A fellow congressman of Madison wrote to a friend:

> Mr. Madison has introduced his long expected amendments. They are the fruit of much labor and research. He has hunted up all the grievances and complaints of newspapers, all the articles of conventions and the small talk of their debates. . . . Upon the whole, it may do some good towards quieting men who attend to sounds

FEDERALIST #10 AND FACTIONALISM

In Federalist #10, James Madison outlines the need for and principles of a democratic republic. Today, many people believe that our government is overly influenced by political parties, interest groups, and other factions. The following excerpt from Federalist #10 *of* The Federalist Papers *highlights Madison's belief in a government able to control factions.*

"Among the numerous advantages promised by a well-constructed union, none deserves to be more accurately developed than its tendency to break and control the violence of faction. The friend of popular governments never finds himself so much alarmed for their character and fate as when he contemplates their propensity of this dangerous vice. . . .

If a faction consists of less than a majority, relief is supplied by the republican principle, which enables the majority to defeat its sinister views, by regular vote. It may clog the administration, it may convulse the society; but it will be unable to execute and mask its violence under the forms of the Constitution. When a majority is included in a faction, the form of popular government, on the other hand, enables it to sacrifice to its ruling passion or interest, both the public good and the rights of other citizens. To secure the public good, and private rights, against the danger of such a faction, and at the same time to preserve the spirit and the form of popular government, is then the great object to which our inquiries are directed. . . .

[I]t clearly appears, that the same advantage, which a republic has over a democracy, in controlling the effects of faction, is enjoyed by a large over a small republic—is enjoyed by the union over the states composing it. . . . The influence of factious leaders may kindle a flame within the particular states, but will be unable to spread a general conflagration through the other states; a religious sect may degenerate into a political faction in a part of the confederacy; but the variety of sects dispersed over the entire face of it, must secure the national councils against any danger from that source: a rage for paper money, for an abolition of debts, for an equal division of property, or for any other improper or wicked project, will be less apt to pervade the whole body of the union than a particular member of it."

only, and may get the mover some popularity, which he wishes.[159]

Madison suggested that the changes be made to the text of the Constitution, but the strongest supporters of the Constitution worried that making changes to the original document would enable a broader revision of the document. This might weaken the fragile unanimity that had been formed by allowing people to continue to criticize other provisions and debate the Constitution's merits all over again. Thus, Roger Sherman proposed that the amendments be added as new and separate articles.

The House approved all of Madison's seventeen amendments and sent them to the Senate, where they were whittled down to fourteen. The conference committee, a committee with members of both houses of Congress formed to agree on the final language of the amendments, further reduced the number to be proposed to the states to twelve.

The Bill of Rights Is Ratified

The states rejected the first two amendments proposed by Congress. One would have regulated the number of representatives in Congress, and the other would have barred any pay raises for congressmen during their terms of office. Both were considered unnecessary. The amendment barring pay raises was ratified in 1992—more than two hundred years after it was introduced—and became the Twenty-seventh Amendment.

The remaining ten amendments were adopted as the Bill of Rights. The Bill of Rights, which passed ratification in December 1791, protects U.S. citizens' most important liberties. Most of the rights with which Americans are familiar—freedom of speech, freedom of religion, the right to a jury trial, protection from "cruel and unusual punishment"—are encapsulated in the Bill of Rights.

Upon hearing that the Bill of Rights had been ratified, North Carolina scheduled its Constitution ratification convention, becoming the twelfth state to ratify. Six months later, Rhode Island narrowly and reluctantly joined the Union after the new Senate passed a bill breaking off commercial relations between the United States and the tiny state. Since then, thirty-seven other territories have been admitted as states of the United States of America.

Refining the System of Government

From the beginning, the Constitution was inadequate to deal with all of the realities facing the new country. For example, the founding fathers did not foresee the rise of political parties and the impact that this would have on their carefully crafted election process. One of the early changes that was made to the Constitution reacted to this development by altering the way the president and the vice president were elected.

Nor did the framers of the Constitution envision the power of lobbying groups, the rise of the government bureaucracy, or

In reaction to Franklin D. Roosevelt's four consecutive terms in office, the Twenty-second Amendment, which limited a president's terms to two, was added to the Constitution.

the rapid growth of communications. They were men of their time, not of the twenty-first century. Yet, the document they created is able to govern today just as effectively as two hundred years ago. This is due largely to the power of amendment.

In response to specific events and broader trends, the Constitution has proven it is able to change the very system under which the nation is governed. Three amendments—the Twelfth, Twentieth, and Twenty-fifth—fixed procedures regarding the office of the president. The Twenty-second Amendment, which was ratified in 1951 in reaction to Franklin D. Roosevelt's election to four terms as president, limits the number of presidential terms to two. Other amendments changed the nature of the relationship of the people with their government. The Sixteenth Amendment,

for example, gave the national government the right to levy an income tax directly on citizens without apportioning it among the states. The Seventeenth Amendment gave the people direct election of their U.S. Senators. This, too, can be seen as a subtle shift away from the powers assumed by individual state governments.

THE WAR AMENDMENTS

In some cases, amendments have resulted from the inability of the founding fathers to fully resolve issues that threatened the nation. Slavery was one of these issues. The Three-Fifths Compromise and other provisions regarding slavery were like putting a band-aid on a festering wound. In the end, the Civil War resolved the problem that the Constitution could not.

The Civil War almost tore apart the union that had been forged at the Constitutional Convention. Changes to the governing document were needed to accommodate the fundamental changes in society that came about at the end of the war. The Thirteenth, Fourteenth, and Fifteenth Amendments, together called the "war amendments," abolished slavery and bestowed on the nation's black Americans the same rights as granted to all other Americans.

The Fourteenth Amendment, in particular, has had a profound effect on the way our nation is governed. It declares that "No State shall make or enforce any law which shall abridge the privileges or immunities of citizens of the United States, nor shall any State deprive any person of life, liberty, or property, without due process of law; nor deny to any person within its jurisdiction the equal protection of the laws." Basically, the Fourteenth Amendment extends the responsibility for the due process protections of the Fifth Amendment to the states. It protects citizens from arbitrary actions of the states and forces states to respect the protections in the Bill of Rights.

THE EXPANSION OF SUFFRAGE

When the founding fathers met in Philadelphia in 1787, it was a gathering of white males, most of whom were fairly wealthy property owners. They believed in self-governance, but in their minds this meant governance by people like themselves. Although a proposal that the Constitution include a property requirement was rejected, the practice of allowing only white adult males the right to vote went unquestioned for many years.

The first change to the voting requirements in the United States came with the passage of the Fifteenth Amendment in 1870, which guaranteed former slaves and other people of color the right to vote. But some state and local governments found ways to get around the Fifteenth Amendment. Several instituted a poll tax, a tax that a voter has to pay in order to vote, to keep minorities and the poor from exercising their right to vote. In the 1950s, civil rights leaders pointed out the government's failure to protect the rights of blacks and other minorities and lobbied for better guarantees. In an attempt to tear down obstacles to suffrage, the Twenty-fourth Amendment, ratified in 1964, made the poll tax illegal.

Women won the right to vote through the Nineteenth Amendment, ratified in 1920. Prior to this amendment, the state

Women were granted the right to vote in 1920 with the ratification of the Nineteenth Amendment.

Federal Agents empty bottles of illegal liquor during Prohibition, which was initiated by the Eighteenth Amendment.

constitutions restricted suffrage to men or imposed property qualifications for voting that excluded most women.

More recent changes to the Constitution have given residents in the District of Columbia the right to vote in national elections and have lowered the eligible voting age to eighteen.

ATTEMPTS AT SOCIAL REFORM

It has proven to be comparatively easy to make changes to the Constitution's governmental structures through the amendment process, but it is much more difficult to change society. The passage of the war amendments, which conferred upon black Americans all the rights guaranteed under the Constitution, did little to stamp out prejudice. For many years, before the passage of the Twenty-fourth Amendment, the states defied the Constitution, finding

ways to get around the provisions that guaranteed blacks the right to vote. Black Americans and other minorities continue to struggle today to preserve the rights guaranteed to them by the Constitution.

Prohibition—that "experiment noble in motive and far-reaching in purpose"[160]—is another example of how ineffective the Constitution is in bringing about social reform. The Eighteenth Amendment, which initiated Prohibition, was drafted with the specific intent of changing attitudes and lifestyles. Passed in 1919, the Eighteenth Amendment was the culmination of a long crusade against drinking waged by temperance organizations. It declared that "the manufacture, sale, or transportation of intoxicating liquors . . . is hereby prohibited."

At the time the amendment was passed, an estimated ninety-five percent of Americans drank alcohol. Although Prohibition was sold as an attack on drunken and disorderly behavior, it forbade moderate social drinking as well. Prohibition soon proved virtually impossible to enforce. Liquor was carried into the United States from Canada or Mexico, smuggled through America's ports, and distilled in remote parts of the countryside. Speakeasies, establishments that served liquor illegally, sprouted up everywhere. More seriously, the huge profits that could be made through the illegal liquor trade contributed to a surge in organized crime. In 1932, just fourteen years after Prohibition went into effect, it was repealed by the Twenty-first Amendment. Prohibition and its repeal is further testimony to the Constitution's ability to allow the people and their government to make mistakes and to correct them.

JUDICIAL REVIEW

"Custom is the great commentator of human Establishments," wrote Gouverneur Morris. "No Constitution is the same on Paper and in Life."[161] While amendments have changed the Constitution in fundamental ways, judicial review has created additional flexibility in the document and has allowed it to keep pace with the customs of the people through vast changes.

In fact, the words of the Constitution itself have changed very little. Since the Bill

---

THE ADVENT OF JUDICIAL REVIEW

When the Constitution was written, little was said about the judicial branch or its powers. This was largely left to the first administrations. In Marbury v. Madison, *Supreme Court Justice John Marshall declared that it was the "responsibility and duty" of the judiciary to interpret the Constitution and make decisions regarding the constitutionality of congressional and executive actions. In this excerpt from Philip B. Kurland's essay, "The Origins of the National Judiciary," in This* Constitution, *Marshall proclaimed the power of judicial review.*

"If two laws conflict with each other, the courts must decide on the operation of each. So if a law be in opposition to the Constitution; if both the law and the Constitution apply to a particular case, so that the court must either decide that case conformably to the law, disregarding the Constitution; or conformably to the Constitution, disregarding the law, the court must determine which of these conflicting rules governs the case. This is the very essence of judicial duty. If, then, the courts are to regard the Constitution, and the Constitution is superior to any Act of the Legislature, the Constitution, and not such ordinary Act, must govern the case to which they both apply."

of Rights was ratified in 1791, only seventeen amendments have been added. Yet, the interpretation of the words of the Constitution, a process called judicial review, has changed tremendously. Judicial review enables the Supreme Court to strike down federal or state laws that conflict with the Constitution. The premise behind judicial review was outlined in 1803 in *Marbury v. Madison,* which marked the first time the Supreme Court declared an act of Congress unconstitutional. "It is emphatically the province and duty of the judicial department to say what the law is,"[162] said Supreme Court Justice John Marshall.

Judicial review plays a critical role in keeping the Constitution up to date. As Woodrow Wilson put it, "The Supreme Court is a constitutional convention in continuous session."[163] Because changes in interpretation can accommodate social, economic, and political changes that take place in the country, the need for frequent amendment is unnecessary. As judges look to the Constitution for guidance, they look from the perspective of the era in which they live. Their rulings are affected by the cultural norms, beliefs, and standards of their day. As Supreme Court Justice William J. Brennan explains:

> We current justices read the Constitution in the only way we can: as twentieth-century Americans. We look to the history of the time of framing and to the intervening history of interpretation. But the ultimate question must be, what do the words of the text mean in our time? For the genius of the Constitution rests not in any sta-

tic meaning it might have had in a world that is dead and gone, but in the adaptability of its great principles to cope with current problems and current needs.[164]

NATIONAL SUPREMACY

There are several other elements of the Constitution that have contributed to its staying power. Among these is Section 8 of Article I, which gives the national government the power "To make all Laws which shall be necessary and proper for carrying into Execution the Foregoing Powers, and all other Powers vested by this Constitution in the Government of the United States, or in any Department or Officer thereof." This has become known as the "necessary and proper" clause.

Supreme Court Justice John Marshall used the clause to expand the power of the national government in *McCulloch v. Maryland,* an 1819 case that arose when Congress created a national bank. Some states' rights advocates, including Luther Martin, a longtime Antifederalist from Maryland, argued that Congress did not have power to establish such a bank. The Supreme Court unanimously decided that, although the Constitution did not explicitly give Congress the power to create a bank, Congress could do so under the necessary and proper clause as part of its power to regulate the economy. John Marshall wrote of the clause:

> This provision is made in a constitution intended to endure for ages to

Judicial Review and Federalist #78

In Federalist #78, *Alexander Hamilton defends the provisions for the judiciary in the Constitution and asserts the responsibility of the courts in determining the meaning of the Constitution as fundamental law. The following excerpt from* Federalist #78 *of* The Federalist Papers *outlines the doctrine of judicial review.*

"The complete independence of the courts of justice is peculiarly essential in a limited constitution. By a limited constitution, I understand one which contains certain specified exceptions to the legislative authority; such, for instance, as that it shall pass no bills of attainder, no *ex post facto* laws, and the like. Limitations of this kind can be preserved in practice no other way than through the medium of courts of justice, whose duty it must be to declare all acts contrary to the manifest tenor of the constitution void. Without this, all the reservations of particular rights or privileges would amount to nothing. . . .

The interpretation of the laws is the proper and peculiar province of the courts. A constitution is, in fact, and must be regarded by the judges as, a fundamental law. It therefore belongs to them to ascertain its meaning as well as the meaning of any particular act proceeding from the legislative body. If there should happen to be an irreconcilable variance between the two, that which has the superior obligations and validity ought, of course, to be preferred; or, in other words, the Constitution ought to be preferred to the statute, the intention of the people to the intention of their agents."

Alexander Hamilton recognized the need for courts to interpret the meaning of the Constitution.

come, and consequently, to be adapted to the various crises of human affairs. To have prescribed the means by which government should, in all future time, execute its powers, would have been to change, entirely, the character of the instrument, and give it the properties of a legal code. It would have been an unwise attempt to provide, by immutable rules, for exigencies which, if foreseen at all, must have been seen dimly, and which can be best provided for as they occur.[165]

The necessary and proper clause has enabled the government to grow and change to accommodate current circumstances. Many functions of government, such as those carried out by the Environmental Protection Agency, the Nuclear Regulatory Agency, or the Air Force, could not have been foreseen by the Constitution's framers. They are made possible by implied powers.

AN ENDURING LEGACY

The U.S. Constitution broke from tradition. Although there had been written

As part of his study of American politics, the French political philosopher Alexis de Tocqueville wrote glowingly about how smoothly the Constitution came into being.

constitutions before, Americans were the first to grant sovereignty to their constitution—to set their constitution above the government. The U.S. Constitution has changed the way people have viewed their contract with government. Before the American Revolution, a constitution referred simply to the way a government operated, but the founding fathers changed all that. By the end of the eighteenth century, Americans viewed a constitution as a document that ceded power to the people. A constitution was not government, but was above government—it was, in the words Gouverneur Morris inserted into his draft, the "law of the land."

The significance of the Constitution also lies in the process by which it was created. Alexis de Tocqueville, who wrote about his observations of America in the 1830s, summed up the unique way in which the Constitution came into being:

> It is new in the history of society, to see a great people turn a calm and scrutinizing eye upon itself, when apprised by the legislature that the wheels of its government are stopped, to see it carefully examine the extent of the evil, and patiently wait two whole years while a remedy is discovered, to which it voluntarily submitted without its costing a tear or a drop of blood from mankind.[166]

Only time will tell how long the Constitution will survive, but it has outlasted all others. Of the more than 170 written constitutions in the world today, the U.S. Constitution is the oldest. It has survived extraordinary expansion and population growth, as well as a civil war, two world wars, and many smaller wars and skirmishes. It has stood steadfastly as the United States has grown from a fledgling nation to a world superpower. While firm, it has not been unyielding. Though amendments and interpretation have changed some of the provisions written more than two hundred years ago, the fundamental principles on which the nation was founded remain intact. Americans continue to look to the Constitution for guidance about how to forge a more perfect union.

Notes

Introduction: The American Experiment

1. Quoted in Catherine Drinker Bowen, *Miracle at Philadelphia*. Boston: Little, Brown and Company, 1986, p. 88.

2. Madison, *Federalist #51*, in *The Federalist Papers*. New York: Bantam Books, 1982, p. 262.

3. Quoted in Bowen, *Miracle at Philadelphia*, p. 242.

Chapter 1: Settling the New World

4. Quoted in "Captain John Smith," Association for the Preservation of Virginia Antiquities, 1997–1998. www.apva.org/history/jsmith.html.

5. Quoted in Winthrop D. Jordan and Leon F. Littwack, *The United States*. 7th ed. Englewood Cliffs, NJ: Prentice-Hall, 1991, p. 21.

6. Quoted in Oscar and Lilian Handlin, *Liberty and Power: 1600–1760*. New York: Harper & Row, 1986, p. 58.

7. Quoted in Francis Newton Thorpe, ed., *The Federal and State Constitutions, Colonial Charters, and Other Organic Laws of the States, Territories, and Colonies Now or Heretofore Forming the United States of America*. Washington, DC: Government Printing Office, 1909.

8. Quoted in Oscar and Lilian Handlin, *Liberty and Power*, p. 73.

9. Hugh Brogan, *The Penguin History of the United States of America*. New York: Penguin Books, 1990, pp. 39–40.

10. From the Virginia Company Records, quoted in Oscar and Lilian Handlin, *Liberty and Power*, p. 57.

11. Oscar and Lilian Handlin, *Liberty and Power*, p. 60.

12. Quoted in James MacGregor Burns et al., *Government by the People*. 16th ed. Englewood Cliffs, NJ: Prentice-Hall, 1995, pp. 11–12.

13. Daniel J. Boorstin, *The Landmark History of the American People: From Plymouth to Appomattox*. New York: Random House, 1987, p. 52.

14. Quoted in Richard Hofstadter, *America at 1750: A Social Portrait*. New York: Random House, 1973, p. 31.

Chapter 2: The American Spirit

15. Quoted in Brogan, *The Penguin History of the United States of America*, p. 138.

16. Quoted in Edmund S. Morgan, *The Birth of the Republic: 1763–89*. Chicago: University of Chicago Press, 1977, p. 5.

17. Quoted in Brogan, *The Penguin History of the United States of America*, p. 71.

18. Benjamin Franklin, *Autobiography, Poor Richard, and Letter Writings*. New York: Library of America, 1997, p. 691.

19. Quoted in Page Smith, *A New Age Now Begins, Volume I*. New York: McGraw-Hill, 1976, p. 240.

20. Quoted in Morgan, *The Birth of the Republic*, p. 17.

21. Quoted in Frank M. Fahey and Marie L. Fahey, *Chapters from the American Experience: Volume One*. Englewood Cliffs, NJ: Prentice-Hall, 1971, p. 130.

22. Department of Humanities Computing, University of Groningen, "Resolutions of the Stamp Act Congress." Text prepared for The American Revolution—an HTML project, 1997. www.let.rug.nl/~usa/D/1751–1775/stampact/sa.htm.

23. Department of Humanities Computing, "Resolutions of the Stamp Act Congress."

24. Quoted in Smith, *A New Age Now Begins*, p. 242.

25. Quoted in Smith, *A New Age Now Begins*, p. 278.

26. Smith, *A New Age Now Begins*, p. 384.

27. Quoted in Oscar and Lilian Handlin, *Liberty in Expansion: 1760–1850.* New York: Harper & Row, 1989, pp. 133–34.

28. Thomas Paine, *Collected Writings.* New York: Library of America, 1995, pp. 25, 28.

29. Smith, *A New Age Now Begins*, p. 682.

30. Quoted in Jim R. McClellan, *Historical Moments: Changing Interpretations of America's Past: Volume I, the Pre-Colonial Period Through the Civil War.* Guilford, CT: The Dushkin Publishing Group, 1994, p. 125.

31. Lance Banning, "From Confederation to Constitution," in *This Constitution: Our Enduring Legacy*, p. 24.

32. Quoted in McClellan, *Historical Moments: Changing Interpretations of America's Past*, p. 125.

Chapter 3: An Attempt at Self-Government

33. Quoted in Brogan, *The Penguin History of the United States of America*, p. 192.

34. Smith, *A New Age Now Begins*, p. 847.

35. Morgan, *The Birth of the Republic*, pp. 88–89.

36. Quoted in Bowen, *Miracle at Philadelphia*, p. 199.

37. Quoted in Dorothy Horton McGee, *Framers of the Constitution.* New York: Dodd, Mead, 1968, p. 12.

38. George Washington, *Writings.* New York: Library of America, 1997, p. 399.

39. Quoted in Smith, *A New Age Now Begins*, p. 566.

40. Washington, *Writings*, p. 352.

41. Washington, *Writings*, pp. 385–86.

42. Quoted in Henry Steele Commager and Richard B. Morris, eds., *The Spirit of 'Seventy-Six.* New York: Harper & Row, 1967, pp. 1,288–89.

43. Quoted in James MacGregor Burns, *The American Experiment: The Vineyard of Liberty.* New York: Alfred A. Knopf, 1982, p. 26.

44. Quoted in Oscar and Lilian Handlin, *Liberty in Expansion*, p. 148.

45. Quoted in Smith, *A New Age Now Begins*, p. 1,762.

46. Quoted in Bowen, *Miracle at Philadelphia*, p. 5.

47. Quoted in Bowen, *Miracle at Philadelphia*, p. 9.

48. Quoted in Morgan, *The Birth of the Republic*, p. 126.

49. Quoted in William Dudley, ed., *The Creation of the Constitution*, San Diego: Greenhaven Press, 1995, p. 28.

50. Quoted in Bowen, *Miracle at Philadelphia*, p. 7.

51. Quoted in Dudley, *The Creation of the Constitution*, p. 28.

52. Quoted in Dumas Malone, *Jefferson and the Rights of Man.* Boston: Little, Brown, 1951, pp. 9, 23.

53. Quoted in Malone, *Jefferson and the Rights of Man*, p. 24.

54. Washington, *Writings*, pp. 621–22.

55. Quoted in Oscar and Lilian Handlin, *Liberty in Expansion*, p. 148.

56. Quoted in Malone, *Jefferson and the Rights of Man*, p. 158.

57. Quoted in Jane Nevins, *Turning 200: A Bicentennial History of the Rise of the American Republic.* New York: Richardson & Steirman, 1987, p. 34.

58. Quoted in Burns et al., *Government by the People*, p. 13.

Chapter 4: The Road to Philadelphia

59. Quoted in Bowen, *Miracle at Philadelphia*, p. 15.

60. Fred Barbash, *The Founding: A Dramatic Account of the Writing of the Constitution*. New York: Linden Press/Simon & Schuster, 1987, p. 18.

61. Quoted in Bowen, *Miracle at Philadelphia*, p. 18.

62. Quoted in Bowen, *Miracle at Philadelphia*, p. 12.

63. Quoted in Nevins, *Turning 200*, p. 38.

64. Quoted in McGee, *Framers of the Constitution*, p. 23.

65. Quoted in McGee, *Framers of the Constitution*, p. 26.

66. Quoted in Bowen, *Miracle at Philadelphia*, p. 44.

67. Oscar and Lilian Handlin, *Liberty in Expansion*, p. 152.

68. Barbash, *The Founding*, p. 47.

69. Burns, *The American Experiment*, p. 33.

70. Madison, *Federalist #51*, p. 262.

71. Oscar and Lilian Handlin, *Liberty in Expansion*, p. 150.

72. Quoted in McClellan, *Historical Moments: Changing Interpretations of America's Past*, p. 142.

73. Quoted in Bowen, *Miracle at Philadelphia*, p. 42.

74. George Mason, letter to his son, quoted in Nevins, *Turning 200*, p. 57.

75. Quoted in Nevins, *Turning 200*, p. 60.

76. Quoted in Nevins, *Turning 200*, p. 60.

77. Quoted in Nevins, *Turning 200*, pp. 61–62; and in Bowen, *Miracle at Philadelphia*, p. 88.

Chapter 5: The Constitutional Convention

78. Quoted in Bowen, *Miracle at Philadelphia*, p. 109.

79. Quoted in Nevins, *Turning 200*, p. 256.

80. Quoted in Nevins, *Turning 200*, p. 69.

81. Quoted in Milton Lomask, *The Spirit of 1787: The Making of Our Constitution*. New York: Farrar Straus Giroux, 1980, p. 117.

82. Bowen, *Miracle at Philadelphia*, p. 38.

83. Quoted in Michael Kammen, ed., *The Origins of the American Constitution: A Documentary History*. New York: Penguin Books, 1986, p. 23.

84. Quoted in Lomask, *The Spirit of 1787*, p. 122.

85. Quoted in Bowen, *Miracle at Philadelphia*, p. 41.

86. Quoted in Burns, *The American Experiment*, p. 35.

87. Quoted in Nevins, *Turning 200*, p. 76.

88. Quoted in Bowen, *Miracle at Philadelphia*, p. 75.

89. Quoted in Bowen, *Miracle at Philadelphia*, p. 80.

90. Quoted in Bowen, *Miracle at Philadelphia*, p. 33.

91. Quoted in Bowen, *Miracle at Philadelphia*, p. 79.

92. Quoted in Nevins, *Turning 200*, p. 122.

93. Quoted in Margot C. J. Mabie, *This Constitution: Reflection of a Changing Nation*. New York: Henry Holt, 1987, pp. 26–28.

94. Quoted in Kammen, ed., *The Origins of the American Constitution*, pp. 54–55.

95. Quoted in Burns, *The American Experiment*, pp. 39–40.

96. Quoted in Lomask, *The Spirit of 1787*, p. 122.

Chapter 6: The Constitution Is Born

97. Quoted in Nevins, *Turning 200*, p. 188.

98. Quoted in James MacGregor Burns and Richard B. Morris, "The Constitution: Thirteen Questions," in *This Constitution: Our Enduring Legacy*. Washington, DC: *Congressional Quarterly*, 1986, p. 7.

99. Quoted in Bowen, *Miracle at Philadelphia*, p. 119.

100. Quoted in Nevins, *Turning 200,* p. 191.

101. Quoted in Malone, *Jefferson and the Rights of Man*, p. 162.

102. Quoted in Burns, *The American Experiment*, p. 37.

103. Hamilton, *Federalist #70*, in *The Federalist Papers*, p. 355.

104. Quoted in Bowen, *Miracle at Philadelphia*, p. 57.

105. Quoted in Nevins, *Turning 200*, pp. 192–93.

106. Forrest McDonald, *A Constitutional History of the United States*. Malabar, FL: Robert E. Krieger, 1986, p. 28.

107. Quoted in Burns, *The American Experiment*, p. 39.

108. Quoted in Burns, *The American Experiment*, p. 39.

109. Quoted in Bowen, *Miracle at Philadelphia*, p. 177.

110. Quoted in Bowen, *Miracle at Philadelphia*, p. 180.

111. Quoted in Bowen, *Miracle at Philadelphia*, p. 179.

112. Quoted in Bowen, *Miracle at Philadelphia*, p. 183.

113. Bowen, *Miracle at Philadelphia*, p. 184.

114. Quoted in Kammen, *The Origins of the American Constitution*, p. 25.

115. Quoted in Bowen, *Miracle at Philadelphia*, pp. 229–30.

116. Quoted in Bowen, *Miracle at Philadelphia*, p. 229.

117. Quoted in Nevins, *Turning 200*, p. 207.

118. Quoted in Bowen, *Miracle at Philadelphia*, p. 232.

119. Quoted in Nevins, *Turning 200*, p. 207.

120. Quoted in Nevins, *Turning 200*, p. 208.

121. Quoted in Bowen, *Miracle at Philadelphia*, p. 259.

122. Quoted in Bowen, *Miracle at Philadelphia*, p. 258.

123. Quoted in McClellan, *Historical Moments: Changing Interpretations of America's Past*, pp. 139–40.

Chapter 7: The Struggle for Ratification

124. Quoted in Bowen, *Miracle at Philadelphia*, p. 259.

125. Quoted in Margot C. J. Mabie, *This Constitution: Reflection of a Changing Nation*. New York: Henry Holt, 1987, p. 52.

126. Quoted in Bowen, *Miracle at Philadelphia*, p. 273.

127. Quoted in Doris Faber and Harold Faber, *We the People: A Story of the United States Constitution Since 1787*. New York: Macmillan, 1987, pp. 51–52.

128. Quoted in McClellan, *Historical Moments: Changing Interpretations of America's Past*, p. 141.

129. Quoted in Lomask, *The Spirit of 1787*, p. 163.

130. Washington, *Writings*, p. 657.

131. Quoted in McClellan, *Historical Moments: Changing Interpretations of America's Past*, p. 141.

132. Quoted in Lomask, *The Spirit of 1787*, p. 167.

133. Quoted in Bowen, *Miracle at Philadelphia*, p. 272.

134. Quoted in Lomask, *The Spirit of 1787*, p. 169.

135. Quoted in Lomask, *The Spirit of 1787*, p. 168.

136. Quoted in Barbash, *The Founding*, p. 210.

137. Quoted in Bowen, *Miracle at Philadelphia*, p. 245.

138. Quoted in Bowen, *Miracle at Philadelphia*, pp. 245–46.

139. Quoted in Nevins, *Turning 200*, p. 271.

140. Quoted in Bowen, *Miracle at Philadelphia*, p. 277.

141. McClellan, *Historical Moments: Changing Interpretations of America's Past*, p. 142.

142. McClellan, *Historical Moments: Changing Interpretations of America's Past*, p. 142.

143. Quoted in Lomask, *The Spirit of 1787*, pp. 189–90.

144. Quoted in Bowen, *Miracle at Philadelphia*, p. 309.

145. Quoted in Richard B. Morris, *The Framing of the Federal Constitution*. Washington, DC: National Park Service, 1986, p. 78.

Chapter 8: An Enduring Legacy

146. Quoted in Bowen, *Miracle at Philadelphia*, p. 263.

147. Quoted in Bowen, *Miracle at Philadelphia*, p. 263.

148. Oscar and Lilian Handlin, *Liberty in Expansion*, pp. 156, 159.

149. Quoted in H. Jefferson Powell, "How Does the Constitution Structure Government? The Founders' Views," in Burke Marshall, ed., *A Workable Government? The Constitution After 200 Years*. New York: W. W. Norton, 1987, p. 18.

150. Quoted in Bowen, *Miracle at Philadelphia*, p. 88.

151. Quoted in McClellan, *Historical Moments: Changing Interpretations of America's Past*, p. 141.

152. Quoted in Mabie, *This Constitution*, p. 89.

153. Quoted in McGee, *Framers of the Constitution*, p. 32.

154. Quoted in Burns, *The American Experiment*, p. 64.

155. Quoted in Nevins, *Turning 200*, p. 335.

156. Quoted in Thomas E. Cronin, "The Origins of the American Presidency," in *This Constitution: Our Enduring Legacy*, p. 80.

157. James Madison, quoted in Nevins, *Turning 200*, p. 335.

158. Quoted in Faber and Faber, *We the People*, p. 69.

159. Quoted in Nevins, *Turning 200*, p. 343.

160. Quoted in Faber and Faber, *We the People*, p. 135.

161. Quoted in Powell, "How Does the Constitution Structure Government?" p. 18.

162. Quoted in Philip B. Kurland, "The Origins of the National Judiciary," in *This Constitution*, p. 89.

163. Quoted in Burns et al., *Government by the People*, p. 38.

164. Quoted in Faber and Faber, *We the People*, p. 13.

165. Quoted in Mabie, *This Constitution*, p. 95.

166. Quoted in McClellan, *Historical Moments: Changing Interpretations of America's Past*, p. 145.

For Further Reading

Mortimer J. Adler, *We Hold These Truths: Understanding the Ideas and Ideals of the Constitution.* New York: Macmillan, 1987. An examination of the principles and philosophies underlying the Constitution.

Akhil Reed Amar, *The Bill of Rights: Creation and Reconstruction.* New Haven, CT: Yale University Press, 1998. Provides information about the history of the Bill of Rights and analysis of the founding fathers' intentions. Chronicles how perceptions of the Bill of Rights have changed over time, focusing particular attention on the impact of the Fourteenth Amendment.

Lydia Bjornlund, *The U.S. Constitution: Blueprint for Democracy.* San Diego: Lucent Books, 1999. A story of the Constitution, focusing on its impact on the United States and on the world.

Donald E. Cooke, *America's Great Document: The Constitution.* Maplewood, NJ: Hammond, 1970. Sets the stage for the Constitutional Convention, depicting Shays's Rebellion, the Annapolis Convention, and the scene in Philadelphia when delegates came together.

Doris Faber and Harold Faber, *The Birth of a Nation.* New York: Charles Scribner's Sons, 1989. A companion to Faber and Faber's *We the People* for younger readers, a briskly moving introduction to constitutional history.

Robert G. Ferris and James H. Charleton, *Signers of the Constitution.* Flagstaff, AZ: Interpretive Publications, 1976. An account that examines the need for the U.S. Constitution, follows the progress of various proposals and debates during the Constitutional Convention, and gives a brief biographical sketch of each of the convention delegates.

Denis J. Hauptly, *A Convention of Delegates: The Creation of the Constitution.* New York: Atheneum Press, 1987. The story of the making of the Constitution, from the end of the Revolutionary War to the ratification by New York.

Nat Hentoff, *American Heroes: In and Out of School.* Delacorte Press, 1987. An examination of the struggles encountered by individuals, from high school students to Supreme Court justices, who have helped keep the Bill of Rights alive.

Forrest McDonald, *We the People: The Economic Origins of the Constitution.* New Brunswick, NJ: Troll Books, 1992. An analysis of how economic factors influenced the making of the Constitution.

Charles L. Mee Jr., *The Genius of the People.* New York: Harper & Row, 1987. A dramatic account of the Constitutional Convention, focusing on the historical background of the Constitution that resulted.

Milton Meltzer, *The American Revolutionaries: A History in Their Own Words.* New York: Crowell, 1987. A detailed account following the events leading up to the call for independence, the American Revolution, the Constitutional Convention, and the ratification debates.

Robert J. Morgan, *James Madison on the Constitution and the Bill of Rights.* Westport, CT: Greenwood Publishing Group, 1988. An analysis of Madison's political philosophy and its effect on the provisions in the Constitution.

Jack N. Rakove, *Declaring Rights: A Brief History with Documents.* New York: Bedford Books, 1997. Discusses development of the Bill of Rights and the Federalists' and Antifederalists' arguments for amending the Constitution. Includes primary documents, letters, declarations, newspaper editorials, and debates.

Works Consulted

Books

Fred Barbash, *The Founding: A Dramatic Account of the Writing of the Constitution.* New York: Linden Press/Simon & Schuster, 1987. An excellent discussion of the people at the 1787 Constitutional Convention and the decisions that they made.

Daniel J. Boorstin, *The Americans: The National Experience.* New York: Random House, 1965. A historical account of the founding of the nation and communities within it.

Daniel J. Boorstin, *The Landmark History of the American People: From Plymouth to Appomattox.* New York: Random House, 1987. A history book written for all readers, covering the major events of early American history.

Catherine Drinker Bowen, *Miracle at Philadelphia.* Boston: Little, Brown, 1986. A highly readable and detailed account of the Constitutional Convention, beginning with the arrival of the delegates in Philadelphia and ending with the ratification of the Constitution.

William Bradford, *On Plimouth Plantation.* New York: Paragon Books, 1962. A firsthand account, written by a community leader, that describes the Pilgrims' experience as they crossed the Atlantic Ocean and settled in Plymouth, Massachusetts.

Hugh Brogan, *The Penguin History of the United States of America.* New York: Penguin Books, 1990. A comprehensive history of the United States, written for common consumption.

James MacGregor Burns, *The American Experiment: The Vineyard of Liberty.* New York: Alfred A. Knopf, 1982. Interweaving historical analysis with vivid biographical portraits, a wide-ranging historical account of the events shaping the republic. Covers the time from the framing of the Constitution to the Emancipation Proclamation.

James MacGregor Burns, J. W. Peltason, Thomas E. Cronin, and David B. Magleby, *Government by the People.* 16th ed. Englewood Cliffs, NJ: Prentice-Hall, 1995. A textbook account of U.S. government.

Henry Steele Commager and Richard B. Morris, eds., *The Spirit of 'Seventy-Six.* New York: Harper & Row, 1967. The story of the American Revolution and the framing of the Constitution as told by participants. Includes letters, speeches, newspaper accounts, pamphlets, and other primary documents from 1776 through ratification of the Constitution.

William Dudley, ed., *The Creation of the Constitution.* San Diego: Greenhaven Press, 1995. Discussions for and against the

Constitution and various aspects included in our Constitution, as written by the people alive during the making and ratification of the document.

Doris Faber and Harold Faber, *We the People: A Story of the United States Constitution Since 1787.* New York: Macmillan, 1987. An account of how the Constitution has governed the United States for two hundred years and how it has accommodated changes in our nation through amendment and Supreme Court decisions.

Frank M. Fahey and Marie L. Fahey, Chapters from the *American Experience: Volume One.* Englewood Cliffs, NJ: Prentice-Hall, 1971. Description of events in early American history, from the colonial days to the mid-1800s. Emphasizes firsthand accounts of those who were there.

Benjamin Franklin, *Autobiography, Poor Richard, and Letter Writings.* New York: Library of America, 1997. A compilation of Franklin's writings, including an autobiography, *Poor Richard's Almanack*, letters, and other documents. Covers material from Franklin's correspondence from London in 1757 to his death.

Joan R. Gunderson and Marshall Smelser, *American History at a Glance.* 5th ed. New York: Harper & Row, 1972. An easy-to-read guide to the pivotal events and issues in America, from the colonial period to the present.

Alexander Hamilton, James Madison, and John Jay, *The Federalist Papers.* New York: Bantam Books, 1982. Contains eighty-five essays written in defense of the Constitution during the ratification debates. A telling look at what the founding fathers intended for our government.

Oscar and Lilian Handlin, *Liberty and Power: 1600–1760.* New York: Harper & Row, 1986. The first of four volumes, an account of America's colonial history.

Oscar and Lilian Handlin, *Liberty in Expansion: 1760–1850.* New York: Harper & Row, 1989. The second of four volumes, an account of America's history, beginning with the events leading up to the American Revolution.

Richard Hofstadter, *America at 1750: A Social Portrait.* New York: Random House, 1973. A description of the colonies in the mid–eighteenth century.

Thomas Jefferson, *Writings.* New York: Library of America, 1984. A compilation of Jefferson's writings, including an autobiography, "Notes on the State of Virginia," public papers, addresses, letters, and other correspondence.

Winthrop D. Jordan and Leon F. Littwack, *The United States.* 7th ed. Englewood Cliffs, NJ: Prentice-Hall, 1991. A textbook account of U.S. history.

Michael Kammen, ed. *The Origins of the American Constitution: A Documentary History.* New York: Penguin Books, 1986. Selections from the constitutional plans, private correspondence of the framers of the Constitution, and Federalist and Antifederalist papers.

Michael Lind, ed., *Hamilton's Republic: Readings in the American Democratic Nationalist Tradition*. New York: Free Press, 1997. Historical account and analysis of the political views that influenced the development of the Constitution and early administrations.

Milton Lomask, *The Spirit of 1787: The Making of Our Constitution*. New York: Farrar Straus Giroux, 1980. An easy-to-read account of the Constitutional Convention, beginning with the "Critical Period" under the Articles of Confederation and ending with ratification of the Constitution.

Margot C. J. Mabie, *This Constitution: Reflection of a Changing Nation*. New York: Henry Holt, 1987. A straightforward account of the Constitution as a framework for government.

Dumas Malone, *Jefferson and the Rights of Man*. Boston: Little, Brown, 1951. The second volume in this Pulitzer Prize–winning six-volume biography. Tells the story of Jefferson during his years in France as the Constitution is developed.

Burke Marshall, ed., *A Workable Government? The Constitution After 200 Years*. New York: W. W. Norton, 1987. Essays on the historical impact of the U.S. Constitution.

Jim R. McClellan, *Historical Moments: Changing Interpretations of America's Past: Volume I, the Pre-Colonial Period Through the Civil War*. Guilford, CT: The Dushkin Publishing Group, 1994. A compilation of primary and secondary sources that reflect on the major events of American history.

Forrest McDonald, *A Constitutional History of the United States*. Malabar, FL: Robert E. Krieger, 1986. A discussion and analysis of the principles and philosophies underlying the Constitution and constitutional issues throughout U.S. history.

Dorothy Horton McGee, *Framers of the Constitution*. New York: Dodd, Mead, 1968. A detailed account of the lives of each of the delegates at the Constitutional Convention. Discusses the background, experiences, and principles of the founding fathers.

Edmund S. Morgan, *The Birth of the Republic: 1763–89*. Chicago: University of Chicago Press, 1977. A short history of the events that transformed the thirteen colonies into a nation, beginning with the events leading up to the American Revolution and ending with the ratification of the Constitution.

Richard B. Morris, *The Framing of the Federal Constitution*. Washington, DC: National Park Service, 1986. The story of the creation and ratification of the federal Constitution, with illustrations and photographs.

Richard B. Morris, *Witnesses at the Creation: Hamilton, Madison, Jay, and the Constitution*. New York: Holt, Rinehart and Winston, 1985. A popular work of history that focuses on the three statesmen's influence on the development and ratification of the Constitution.

Richard B. Morris and James Woodress, eds., *Voices from America's Past, Volume I: The Colonies and the New Nation.* New York: Webster, 1963. The story of America from the eyes of those who were there. Includes diaries, letters, biographies, memoirs, essays, and narratives, with brief introduction and analysis to place them in context. Volume I covers subjects from the founding of Jamestown in 1607 to the administration of John Quincy Adams.

Jane Nevins, *Turning 200: A Bicentennial History of the Rise of the American Republic.* New York: Richardson & Steirman, 1987. An easy-to-read account of the Constitutional Convention, ratifying conventions, and first administration under the new government.

Thomas Paine, *Collected Writings.* New York: Library of America, 1995. "Common Sense," "The Crisis," and other pamphlets, articles, and letters written by statesman Thomas Paine.

Page Smith, *A New Age Now Begins.* New York: McGraw-Hill, 1976. A detailed narrative of the birth of the United States of America in three volumes. Volumes I and II cover the events leading up to and during the American Revolution; Volume II also touches briefly on the making of the Constitution.

This Constitution: Our Enduring Legacy. Washington, DC: *Congressional Quarterly,* 1986. Series of essays on various aspects of the Constitution and its application throughout American history. Written by leading historians and constitutional scholars.

Francis Newton Thorpe, ed., *The Federal and State Constitutions, Colonial Charters, and Other Organic Laws of the States, Territories, and Colonies Now or Heretofore Forming the United States of America.* Washington, DC: Government Printing Office, 1909. Early documents of American history.

George Washington, *Writings.* New York: Library of America, 1997. A compilation of letters and other correspondence written by George Washington from the colonial period to his death.

Internet Sources

Association for the Preservation of Virginia Antiquities, "Captain John Smith," 1997–1998. www.apva.org/history/jsmith.html.

Department of Humanities Computing, University of Groningen, "Resolutions of the Stamp Act Congress," 1997. www.let.rug.nl/~usa/D/1751–1775/stampact/sa.htm.

Index

Picture Credits

Cover photo: North Wind Picture Archives

Archive Photos, 15

Dover Publications, Inc., 26, 29, 35, 44, 63, 70, 71, 77, 79, 81, 93, 110

Independence National Historical Park Collection, 61

Library of Congress, 10, 24, 25, 27, 32, 34, 36, 37, 39, 40, 43, 47, 55, 57, 62, 65, 67, 68, 73, 74 (bottom), 78, 82, 85, 87, 89, 100, 104, 105, 106, 109

North Wind Picture Archives, 19, 74 (top)

Joseph Paris Picture Archive, 30

Stock Montage, Inc., 14, 50, 98

About the Author

Lydia Bjornlund is a private consultant and freelance writer, focusing primarily on issues related to civic education, government, and training. She is the author of more than a dozen books and training manuals, as well as numerous magazine and newsletter articles.

Ms. Bjornlund holds a master of education degree from Harvard University and a bachelor of arts from Williams College, where she majored in American studies. She lives in Oakton, Virginia, with her husband Gerry Hoetmer and their three cats.